"Genuine friendship is one of the most important elements in lasting ministry. Finally we have a book that teaches this eternal principle for longevity. *Leaders That Last* is a godsend to ministry leaders. Gary Kinnaman and Alfred Ells use lessons form their personal friendship and ministry to make a compelling case for acquiring and maintaining healthy pastoral relationships. Readers will be challenged to pray for friends who can help them survive the rigors of ministry."

Ted Haggard, senior pastor, New Life Church, Colorado Springs

"I practice what they preach and believe it to be the single best idea to preserve pastors because it is pragmatic and effective. Read and apply to stay in the race."

Dr. Alan Nelson, founder, Leading Ideas; author, *Spirituality and Leadership*

"Jesus defined life as relational, and it is in relationship with him and others that we find the abundant life he promised. *Leaders That Last* gives the account of one successful pastor who has actually found the enjoyment of this life in ministry. This book will be a great encouragement."

Darryl DelHousaye, senior pastor, Scottsdale Bible Church;
president, Phoenix Seminary

"Dr. Gary Kinnaman combines a humble heart and a remarkable comprehension of other cultures beyond his own. His ministry is a treasure of God that will profoundly enrich the Hispanic community. I recommend him with all my heart."

Alberto H. Mottesi, evangelist

"One of the great needs in the world today is summed up in the title *Leaders That Last*. Gary Kinnaman and Al Ells have examined this subject from the unique vantage point of having dealt personally with both leaders that have lasted and, tragically, those who haven't. Their collective insight, wisdom, and advice in this work should become required reading for today's leaders—and tomorrow's."

Tommy Barnett, pastor, Phoenix First Assembly of God

"Large-church culture is full of frequent, predictable, painful problems (small churches have their own). In *Leaders That Last*, Gary (a megachurch pastor) and Al (a therapist and consultant) open up about these faults. Their thoughtful candor is "sane" advice (especially their tips for groups) for healing "insane," unsafe church cultures and the people who—in spite of a pastor's best efforts—create them."

Todd Hunter, director, Allelon Fellowship of Churches;
former national director, Vineyard-USA

"Covenant groups for busy and drained leaders is a win-win idea, and this book is a vital resource for pastors considering accountability with relationships. It is a great book with awesome stories and will be used to save many ministries from extinction."

Frank Damazio, senior pastor, City Bible Church, Portland, Oregon

"The local church has a vital role to play in contemporary society, and its leaders are often the determining factor for success or failure. For too long we've seen many leaders going at it alone or dropping out of the race prematurely. This book is a clarion call to church leaders to begin cultivating the kind of friendships that will help ensure that they are 'leaders that last.'"

Mark Conner, senior pastor, Waverley Christian Fellowship, Melbourne, Australia

"This book comes at a very critical time of transition for the church. Without a doubt the contents of this book bring a voice of stability and hope for many pastors and leaders across America. Both Gary and Al are personal friends and mentors whose teachings have greatly influenced my life and ministry. The message within this pages will challenge you to take the next step for a kingdom vision that will transform your life and your ministry."

Hector Torres, Hispanic International Ministries

"I love to learn from leaders I trust. In *Leaders That Last*, Gary Kinnaman has given us the treasures of his life. If we ponder these words and walk in this wisdom, our lives will be rescued from great folly and set on paths of joy."

John Dawson, president, YWAM International

"Every leader of a growing ministry and every pastor of a local church will immediately identify with the heartfelt insights of Gary Kinnaman and Alfred Ells. *Leaders That Last* goes right to the heart of the pressures leaders face, coping mechanisms that can undermine our ministry, and how to develop the health and skill necessary to finish well. It is the most effective and insightful book I have read in many years on the heart of a spiritual leader."

Floyd McClung, director, All Nations; senior pastor,
Metro Christian Fellowship, Grandview, Missouri

"Church leaders carry enormous loads, and all too often they do it alone. Without close friends, trusted confidants, or genuine supporters, many of them eventually wear out under the pressure of ministry. This book provides wise, practical, and biblical advice on how to build the safe relationships and godly accountability that church leaders need in order to persevere and thrive in pastoral ministry."

Ken Sande, president, Peacemaker Ministries

Leaders *That* Last

Leaders
That Last

How Covenant Friendships Can Help Pastors Thrive

Gary D. Kinnaman
and Alfred H. Ells

Baker Books

A Division of Baker Book House Co
Grand Rapids, Michigan 49516

© 2003 by Gary D. Kinnaman and Alfred H. Ells

Published by Baker Books
a division of Baker Book House Company
P.O. Box 6287, Grand Rapids, MI 49516-6287
www.bakerbooks.com

Printed in the United States of America

Library of Congress Cataloging-in-Publication Data
Kinnaman, Gary D.
        Leaders that last : how covenant friendships can help pastors thrive / Gary
    D. Kinnaman and Alfred H. Ells.
             p.   cm.
        Includes bibliographical references and index.
        ISBN 0-8010-9163-2 (pbk.)
        1. Clergy—Psychology. 2. Clergy—Professional relationships. 3. Friend-
    ship—Religious aspects—Christianity. I. Ells, Alfred. II. Title.
    BV4398.K56 2003
    253'.2—dc22   2003017007

Unless otherwise indicated, Scripture is taken from the HOLY BIBLE, NEW INTERNATIONAL VERSION®. NIV®. Copyright © 1973, 1978, 1984 by International Bible Society. Used by permission of Zondervan. All rights reserved.

Scripture marked KJV is taken from the King James Version of the Bible.

Scripture marked TLB is taken from *The Living Bible* © 1971. Used by permission of Tyndale House Publishers, Inc., Wheaton, IL 60189. All rights reserved.

Scripture marked MESSAGE is taken from THE MESSAGE. Copyright © by Eugene H. Peterson 1993, 1994, 1995. Used by permission of NavPress Publishing Group.

Contents

108176

Introduction

The walls are coming down! As Howard Snyder predicted nearly two decades ago in his landmark book *Foresight,* the church has made an enormous shift away from denominational and institutional traditions toward kingdom mission.

This book is about the next shift—from unity movements and ministry partnerships to genuine friendships and relational accountability among diverse leaders who represent the Christian faith in a given city.

Although C. Peter Wagner's term "postdenominationalism" has not been well-received, it's a fact that denominations, both mainline and conservative, are reeling from the massive social upheavals of the last several decades. Driven by globalization and technological revolution, the times, well, they are a-changin'. New "apostolic" movements are emerging worldwide, and the influence of entrepreneurial megachurches like Willow Creek and Saddleback often transcends denominational models and influence. The huge and influential Promise Keepers men's movement is another sign of transdenominational times.

A parallel trend has been a widespread interest in "city-reaching," in which churches and ministries in cities across America are coming together to work for spiritual renewal and community transformation.

Thus we see two significant opportunities facing the church in the twenty-first century. First, local churches *must* work together in an increasingly hostile, post-Christian world. The apostle Paul's teaching about the members of the body of Christ isn't just about what happens in a local church. It's about all of us, including those in divergent leadership contexts, working together and understanding that we need one another in order for the church to be the church. If Paul were writing 1 Corinthians 12:21 today, he might say something like this: "The Baptists can't say to the Lutherans, 'I don't need you,' the Nazarene pastor can't say to the Pentecostal pastor across town, 'I don't need you,' and the megachurch pastor can't say to the pastor of the small church down the street, 'I don't need you!'"

Second, those of us in full-time ministry need significant and safe relationships to strengthen and sustain us in an increasingly difficult vocation. Now more than ever, we need each other "professionally" because we have a shared mission, but we need one other "personally" as well. We won't survive—and our churches won't survive—if we don't invest in long-term, transformational relationships with one another.

Leaders don't seem to be lasting. According to one study, some fifteen hundred pastors leave the ministry every month, and most never return. Although this is an extraordinarily complex issue involving multiple factors, we are convinced that the primary problem is this: Most people in full-time ministry do not have close personal friendships and consequently are alarmingly lonely and dangerously vulnerable.

Why is it so difficult for church leaders to overcome their suspicions and insecurities to become friends and work together? Do we really know what it means to love one another as much as we say we love Jesus? Pastors are discovering that we are not enemies or even competitors. But are we willing to make the kind of covenant commitment to one another that will allow us to stand together when one of us is hurting? How about when one us falls? Those of us in ministry are "colleagues" (a safe and sterile term), but can we be closer than brothers? Are we men and women with many acquaintances and casual friendships, or can we say we have a friend or two "who sticks closer than a brother" (Prov. 18:24)?

This book is about the possibility of forming those kinds of friendships between those of us in full-time ministry. It's also about the potential of deep, covenant relationships to change us, to renew our churches, and to transform our communities. We know it can happen because we've seen it happen. What we have to say is deeply rooted in our personal stories.

A counselor, educator, and organizational consultant for decades, Al has served hundreds of leaders and scores of churches and ministries. He and Gary have been close personal friends for nearly twenty years, a relationship that began when Gary and his church were in crisis.

Gary is Al's pastor, and Al served for many years on the governing board of Gary's church, Word of Grace, a nondenominational fellowship in Mesa, Arizona. Since its birth in 1980, the church has grown to an average weekend attendance of over forty-five hundred adults and children. In addition to serving as senior minister of Word of Grace, Gary has been uniquely qualified to build bridges of unity and ministry partnerships in the Greater Phoenix area.

Am I Crazy?

Eighty percent of pastors and eighty-four percent of their spouses are discouraged or are dealing with depression.

—Focus on the Family

I'm no longer in denial. I'm in burnout.

—A pastor friend

The darkest hour of the dark night of my soul. That's how I (Gary) describe it to my friends. Nowhere to go. No one to help. Sink or swim.

Maybe God didn't call me to the ministry. Maybe I should just quit. I could never take my own life, but right now I'd rather be dead than dying this slow death. I know Jesus wants me to pay the price, but this is just too much for me and my family to bear.

These were my feelings about fifteen years ago when our small movement of independent churches crashed and burned. In a matter of months, lifelong friends and associates, elders and church members became embroiled in a multichurch conflict that affected the lives of thousands of people.

My depression was suffocating, and then I came down with a heart problem. No cardiologist was able to tell me exactly what was wrong, although one top diagnostician told me cautiously that I had cardiomyopathy.

"What's *that?*" I asked.

Glancing up at me from behind my medical chart, he rolled his eyes just above the rim of his reading glasses and, deadpanning, informed me, "Cardiomyopathy is a weakening of the heart. We don't know what causes it. Maybe a virus. And we have no cure."

Later I found out that cardiomyopathy is the kiss of death. At least insurance companies think so; getting life insurance with cardiomyopathy on your medical record is impossible. It's the heart disease people have when they need a transplant.

Just before that dreadful year was over, two people on my church staff died—one of a vicious cancer, the other in an automobile accident in northern New Mexico. I did two *staff* funerals back to back on the last two days of 1987.

And then there was all the analysis. How God's people interpreted and misinterpreted these events could have been the inspiration for a science fiction novel. Ironically, I live in an Arizona city bounded on the east by an imposing range of craggy, crimson mountains, the Superstitions. You've probably seen them in Western movies. So we have a Superstition Freeway. And a Superstition Mall. I thought, tongue in cheek, that we probably should have a Superstition Christian Center too.

If we're not wrestling with flesh and blood, why does it feel like the people we're serving are killing us? And why do so many of us in ministry feel like we're dying inside? Why is the level of "job" dissatisfaction so high among members of the clergy? And why are so many of us depressed?

Focus on the Family recently reported that approximately fifteen hundred pastors are leaving their assignments each month due to moral failure, spiritual burnout, or contention in their local congregations, and according to *Pastor's Weekly Briefing,*[1] pressures on pastors are greater than once thought. Psychologist Richard Blackmon, in an article in the *Los Angeles Times*, claims that "pastors are the single most occupationally frustrated group in America."[2] About 75 percent go through periods of stress so great that they consider quitting the ministry.[3]

It's staggering.

The myriad glitzy spiritual renewal and church growth conferences advertised in Christian magazines often mask the pain of the thousands of leaders who attend only to face the same-old-same-old when they return to their churches and homes.

Why is ministry so terribly difficult? Why do the statistics tell us that it's the toughest vocation on earth? Is there more to it than, well, just more prayer? Why aren't the standard answers working?

■ A Christian Culture of Denial

The job itself is tough enough, but to make matters worse, much worse, we pastors and Christian leaders live and work in a subculture where failure disqualifies us. No, I'm not just talking about an affair with your secretary. Your failure may be negligible, like one bad sermon or one crabby moment in the lobby of the worship center. Or it may be an *imagined* failure, like the pastor I heard about whose child was diagnosed with a terminal illness and died. For reasons well outside the circle of God's grace and love, his congregation just couldn't deal with it. Like Job's counselors, people in his church came to the conclusion that his child's illness was somehow his fault, a consequence of some spiritual shortcoming in his life. He's not the pastor of that church anymore.

If there is a *real* failure, like a sexual failure, or something far less consequential like depression (I have that), we are reluctant, even afraid, to talk about it. So we suffer silently until one day, when it may be too late to do much about it, the problem goes public. Or we just crash. And everyone around us wonders, *Where did* that *come from? I thought my pastor had it all together.*

■ Convoluted Conflicts in the Church

The conflicts I have experienced personally are shamefully common in local churches regardless of worship style or denominational affiliation. They are the power points of spiritual warfare, hell's declaration of the death of a congregation.

The issues in any conflict are often as murky as what they call "June gloom" in San Diego. Every church fight is a fight for, well, no one really knows, but everyone is really angry. Few, though, will admit to being angry, because that's not Christian. Instead, people are "righteously indignant," usually for something they think God is mad about too. In fact, I've come to observe that, at least in charismatic churches, *no one* ever gets angry about *anything*. They just prophesy to one another!

Church conflict is not unlike Acts 19:32, which in fact describes a pagan riot in Ephesus: "The assembly was in confusion: Some were shouting one thing, some another. *Most of the people did not even know why they were there*" (italics mine).

We wrestle not with flesh and blood, yet that is exactly what happens in our local churches. People problems are everywhere; and most people involved have little or no recognition that *all of us,* regardless of what side we're on, are vulnerable to spiritual deception. We point holy fingers instead of seeing the problems for what they are, instead of *all of us* taking responsibility for our complicity in those problems, instead of resisting the devil in the process.

It seems like we wrestle much more with each other than we do with the devil. We devote more time to defending ourselves and arguing why our side is right than we do to praying and to relentlessly committing to work through our misunderstandings in an appropriate manner.

Or to put it another way: There's never a problem until there's a problem. In other words, the most basic of all problems—in church, in families, in me—is not any particular problem, but what happens in me and among us when problems arise. "Trials of many kinds" (the particular kind doesn't matter!) test our character and faith. Problems just bring up deeper problems. The problem is never the problem; it's what we do with it. Things happen. "Offences will come" (Luke 17:1 KJV). Conflict is common. Carnal responses to conflict are common. What is uncommon is the managing and resolving of conflict in a godly way.

Like a brand-new marriage, everything in a good and growing church will seem just perfect—until there is a problem. That problem then becomes the proverbial test to see what's really inside of us—a lot of Jesus or mostly me. Then and only then, in the heat of the fire, do we discover how spiritually immature and ill-equipped for deep relationship we really are. If you want to know what a person is really like, watch him or her carefully under pressure. Every difficulty forces us to decide whether we will accede to the conflict or have the courage and faith to persevere until the problem is resolved and both or all the people are reconciled.

■ Preaching What We Aren't

The challenges of Christian ministry are, humanly speaking, impossible to overcome. We surely need the love and strength of God to sustain us in the battle, but we also need one another. It's what best-selling author Steven Covey calls "interdependence." For theologian Martin Buber it was the interface of I-and-Thou; and twentieth-century martyr Dietrich Bonhoeffer wrote about it in his extraordinary little book on the Christian community, *Life Together.* We need each other.

Ah, the body of Christ! We pastors preach about it. We teach on how every member has a part to play, and we encourage our people to embrace one another in love. So why can't they all just get along?

Could it be that *we* are part of the problem? Why can't we Christian leaders all just get along? Why are we so alienated from one another? Are doctrinal and denominational walls keeping us apart? I think not, because pastors and leaders *within* denominations are isolated from one another as well.

Al and I are convinced that pastors are not just victims of the subculture of the church; we are the ones who create and

sustain that culture. The culture of the church is often superfi-
cial and artificial, even dysfunctional, because we pastors are
all of those things, and the Christian community can never be
anything more or less than what we model.

■ Changing the Way We Think about Change

I know this is terribly troubling, but even our model of
change is dysfunctional. As I once heard Christian social activ-
ist John Perkins agonize, "We, the church, have told the world
what's important by how we spend our money. Words [rhetoric]
are more important to us than anything else, because that's
how we spend our money." Radio and television. Publications
(this book!). Buildings designed for talking. Words, words, and
more words. And we wonder why there's no revival, why the
church doesn't really change.

Much as I hate to think about this, researcher George Barna
found that sermons (words, talk) are changing people in the
pews only a very little. He found instead that the most powerful
change factors in human life are crises and accountable mentoring relationships.

Words *are* important! That's why we're writing this book.
That's why Paul asked rhetorically, "How can they hear without
a preacher?" If words aren't important, why the Bible? It's God's
Word and words. But real change occurs not merely because
someone hears me preach or reads this book.

The Bible is alive. God himself speaks through it, and the
power of his Spirit is released when we read it. But even the
Bible makes it clear that real personal growth comes through
doing the Word, not just hearing it. We grow as the Word
becomes real to us in the contexts of life. It's that old "count
it all joy" stuff. Difficulties in life are the fertile fields where
character grows. People change when truth is experienced and
tested in the milieu of life. People change, as it has been said,
when the pain to change becomes less than the pain to remain
the same. This is what happened in my (Gary's) life.

If you don't think this is true, why do you discipline your children? Do parents actually believe their children will change just because they tell them something is right or wrong? Furthermore, do preachers actually believe people will change just because they tell them something is right or wrong?

My pastor friend John Vawter loves golf. Not too long ago I made a comment about his sweater, which was emblazoned with the Native American–like name of a local golf course: Talking Stick. With his wry wit, John responded, "I point to this when people ask me what I do for a living." John was implying, of course, that so much of the ministry seems like "just talk."

■ Modeling What "the Church Is Meant to Be"

How can we as Christian leaders, for example, just *talk* about reconciliation and open relationships when we are some of the most isolated people on God's earth? How can we call people into submission and accountability when we are, essentially, accountable to no one? How can we expect people in our churches to be a part of small groups when we ourselves are not in small groups? "Community" is a prominent theme in the church today, but what do we leaders know about community personally?

In 1997 best-selling Christian author Larry Crabb, who advocates the power of groups over one-on-one counseling, published his groundbreaking book *Connecting*, followed by *The Safest Place on Earth* in 1999. In the foreword to Crabb's second book, Eugene Peterson says, "Most of us assume that, having decided to follow Jesus as our Lord and Savior, we will find ourselves in a spiritual community of like-minded friends, a family of brothers and sisters, enjoying one another's companionship on our way to glory. More often than not we are disappointed."[4]

The cover flap of *The Safest Place on Earth* announces:

> Dr. Crabb addresses this universal failure of the church head-on and leads us toward a profound new vision of what the

church can be—indeed, was meant to be. Rather than a place
for people to display their goodness and hide their failures in
fear of censure, the church should be open, supportive, and
compassionate in dealing with our weaknesses. It should be
"the safest place on earth."[5]

Al and I are convinced, though, that the Christian community
will never "become mature, attaining to the whole measure of
the fullness of Christ" (Eph. 4:13) unless leaders in the church
model community themselves. The isolation of pastors from
their people and from one another is the Great Barrier Reef
between the ocean of God's love and the vast, sterile continent
of organized religion. Something has to change radically in the
Christian leadership community before significant change can
happen in the Christian community at large. We've said it for
years: "It's better caught than taught."

If I model holiness, people will become holier. If I model
giving, people will give. If I model Bible study or prayer or
something simple like courteous behavior, people will watch
and follow. Less than perfectly I've done all that, but it's only
in recent years that I've found myself modeling "what the
church was meant to be," a safe community of life-changing
relationships.

And how have I done this? I've chosen to model transparency
and the vulnerability that goes with it. I've decided to be open
about my weaknesses. And I've modeled this to one degree
or another in virtually every relationship in my life, from the
pulpit of my church, but especially in intentional relationships
with other pastors.

■ But for the Grace of God

What has been amazing to me is that my vulnerability has
actually deepened the trust others have in me instead of doing
what everybody in ministry seems to fear—that is, if you let
down your guard, people will think less of you. I'm quite sure
this is what the apostle Paul was getting at when he said,

"Therefore I will *boast* all the more gladly about *my weaknesses,* so that Christ's power may rest on me. That is why, for Christ's sake, *I delight in weaknesses* [How weird would that be in most churches?], in insults, in hardships, in persecutions, in difficulties. For when I am weak, then I am strong" (2 Cor. 12:9–10, italics mine).

You see, when I am strong, and I tell you about that, you may very well, without really thinking about it, follow *me.* I become your example more than Jesus—so much so that if I fail or fall, you will likely crash with me. But when I am weak, and I tell you about that, about how I struggle with all the things you struggle with, and about how God's grace is sufficient for me, you will be deeply and greatly encouraged. You will find yourself saying, if God can love and use Gary, he can use me!

That's how I personally feel about the apostle Paul! Jesus is my Savior, but Paul is my hero: Chief of sinners. Religious to a fault. Angry and argumentative. And Jesus could use him? Wow! At least I have never started a riot in my city, although I have been known to get out of hand at board and staff meetings.

■ Leaders Going Deeper

If your experience is like mine, you have probably become acquainted with other pastors and Christian leaders in your area as a result of some event or task. It may have been something as basic and as important as prayer, but it was nevertheless a task. Regardless of how many ministerial associations we join or how many pastors' luncheons we attend, we leaders continue to dance and court without ever really making a serious commitment to one another to be long-term, accountable friends. Is it possible, and I say this tongue-in-cheek, for us to be friends, to spend time with one another, even when Billy Graham is not coming to town for a citywide crusade?

Al and I contend that pastors who meet with their boards, their staff, or their friends in the church are in groups that by their inherent boundaries create relationships with limits. Just meeting with people is not necessarily a mechanism for growth. This, in fact, is affirmed by the findings of the Fuller Institute: Even though pastors know and meet with many people, 70 percent of the pastors surveyed reported that they do not have someone they consider a close friend.[6] In the January 2000 issue of *Ministries Today*, H. B. London of Focus on the Family said the number was over 80 percent.[7]

Not too long ago, Al was asked to speak at a small, regional gathering of pastors from a major denomination. As he shared openly about some of his own very personal issues, one of the men in the room began to weep uncontrollably about his very serious marriage problems. No one else in the room, not one of his forty colleagues, had a clue that this brother was dying inside and on the verge of leaving the ministry.

He couldn't tell his deacons, because his effectiveness in ministry could have been greatly undermined. He couldn't tell his area leader, his district superintendent, or his bishop, because he could have risked losing his job. And if none of that could happen, how could he possibly let his people know that his marriage was failing? Oh, the shame of it. So he told no one.

Or consider my friend Phil. Raised in a pastor's family, Phil felt he had little choice but to become one himself. But what he saw in his very traditional and conservative denomination led to disillusionment and a repositioning of himself in a very different kind of church. He made the radical shift from a Pentecostal-style of ministry to seeker-driven.

But Phil's definition of "pastor" didn't change. He still found himself walking the tightrope between what people expected him to be and what he *really* was. And even though his church was doing *really* well, Phil was *really* depressed and nearing burnout.

Providentially, I was with Phil in our pastors' covenant group the morning of the same day he was scheduled to see his doctor. New in our group, he very cautiously shared his pain. He was relieved that none of us in the room reacted with surprise. None of us tried to "fix" him with Bible verses, either. We just listened and prayed. And I did a startling thing—me, the big-time, successful pastor. I confessed to him that I had taken medication for depression.

Silence. Prayer. Tears.

Actually, it wasn't so tough for me to talk about my depression. I'd gotten past most of my inhibitions in that regard. But Phil had never heard anything like it, because talking about those kinds of things is taboo in much of the Christian community. We can pray publicly in the services for Harold in the hospital with hepatitis, but if Harold is just plain depressed all the time, he should go to the men's retreat. A little more of God and he should snap right out of it.

Or will he?

Later Phil wrote to me, "I can't tell you how liberating it was for me to know that I was not the only Christian leader suffering from serious depression. Or that I could actually talk about it safely with other pastors. It was a turning point in my life, and it made me realize how necessary it was for me to be in a committed relationship with all of you." Just last week Phil told me he was going to be able to go off the medication.

The article in *Pastor's Weekly Briefing* that I mentioned at the beginning of this chapter concludes with simple but uncommonly practiced wisdom: Pastors need to set limits for themselves in order to avoid burnout. The author suggests that to maintain balance we must develop friendships outside the church and create support groups with other religious leaders.[8]

Brothers and sisters, we need each other! We need each other, because pastors are generally private, introspective, introverted, insecure, and even reclusive. Personally, I prefer time with my family and very individualized kinds of hobbies. John Maxwell said once that he likes to collect autographs of great leaders. So do I. And I enjoy working on my model railroad, which I must confess is my alternative universe. There I can glue people down permanently to the plywood, and no one complains. Every time I look at my miniature world, it's exactly the way I left it.

And in more wicked moments, I can rip up those little people, lay them across the electrified tracks, and watch them sizzle. Of course I would not, could not, do that with real people, because I am a pastor! And pastors never have feelings like that about real people.

Or do we?

We need each other, because we are very good at talking. Talking loudly. Talking persuasively. Talking, talking, talking. But we're not very good at listening, because that's what our people are supposed to do when we are talking. "Be quick to listen, slow to speak," James tells all of us "talking sticks" (James 1:19).

We need each other, because pastors are generally authoritarian, not democratic. We may be assertively authoritarian, or we may be very nice, but deep down inside, each of us feels a need to control the church we pastor. Sometimes we even feel a little messianic.

We need each other, because whether or not we want to admit it, hundreds of years of denominational segregation is ending. We are living in what Peter Wagner has termed a "postdenominational era."[9] Not that denominations have served out their useful purpose; it's good to be related institutionally to other churches of similar belief and worship style. But the new century will be characterized by a move away from denominational and institutional traditions to a shared kingdom vision and mission. Indeed, in my city I have experienced a commonality of kingdom purpose among pastors and leaders from nearly every denomination, including a couple of surprisingly evangelical Catholic leaders.

Oh, and my cardiomyopathy? Nearly fifteen years later I'm just fine, although when I'm really tired, the palpitations return as a constant reminder that every breath I breathe is sustained by the presence of the living God. I understand something of what Paul felt when he wrote, "I bear on my body the marks of Jesus" (Gal. 6:17). Or like Jacob, who after wrestling not with flesh and blood at a place called Jabbok, walked with a limp. My suffering has left me with a mark, a Purple Heart for the wounds of spiritual warfare.

Through it all, though, I have discovered the God-given treasure of mature, godly friends who speak the truth to me in love and refuse to let me gag and drown in the swamp of my own self-interest. I couldn't have survived without the love and firm wisdom of people like my coauthor, Al. He'll tell you the story from his perspective in the next chapter.

These Guys Are in Trouble!

Between 30 and 40 percent of surveyed pastors express a desire to leave the pastorate.

—Pulpit & Pew and Focus on the Family

Six thousand Southern Baptist Church pastors leave the ministry each year, and 225 are fired each month.

—Dr. Fred Gage

"I don't know how you do it!" I exclaimed. "Aren't you afraid of burning out? I am concerned that you're heading for disaster if you don't slow down."

These were the words I (Al) shared with Gary ten years ago after a particularly difficult meeting. He had just returned from an overseas missionary trip on Saturday, preached two services that night and three more on Sunday morning. At our early Tuesday morning meeting he was impatient and argumentative.

"Why are you asking me these questions?" he complained. He didn't want to listen or dialogue. He only wanted to give his opinion—over and over again. It was obvious that he didn't have the emotional reserves needed to discuss some of the thornier issues on the agenda.

Gary is the full-time senior pastor of a large, thriving church. He has built the church to more than forty-five hundred weekend attendees. He travels a lot, does multiple services each weekend, and even finished a doctorate degree through Western Conservative Baptist Seminary while pastoring the church full time.

If you ask Marilyn, his wife, about how well Gary handles all the stress, she will say, "Gary gets easily irritated with me and the children." Gary agrees that he is often too impatient, especially when he feels overwhelmed and anxious. He confided in me that there are times when he actually dreads having to preach. You would never know it though. Every Sunday before crowds of thousands, he is animated, humorous, and deeply convicting with his message. He does what every minister does—puts on the "game face" and performs no matter how stressed, upset, or sick he is feeling.

■ Pastoring Is a Difficult Job

Gary obviously has a lot on his plate. Are his demanding workload and personal stress an exception? Is he unusual in that he has substantially more stress and more responsibilities to juggle than other clergy? No, I don't think so.

I'm not only Gary's friend; I'm also a marriage and family therapist and church consultant. I work with clergy and parachurch leaders across North America. I spend my time connecting and working with clergy from many different traditions and churches. I see stress in almost all their lives. Shepherding a church in today's world is extremely difficult. It is hard to meet the complex personal, relational, and organizational challenges clergy must face. Consider, for example, the diversity of gifting and function a minister must master to be successful. He or she must

- understand governance and be able to coach a volunteer board of elders/trustees in their role
- inspirationally lead others
- organize, manage, supervise, and monitor staff—especially volunteer staff
- understand budgets, balance sheets, and fund-raising
- know and work with media
- be an educator, able to teach and have good study skills
- counsel, coach, and give pastoral care
- perform sacerdotal functions with grace
- be a gifted public and private communicator
- be able to appropriately manage and resolve conflict
- authentically represent God
- live a holy life—never sin or fail

No wonder national surveys indicate that ministers are possibly the most frustrated and neglected professional group in the country. They are frustrated with not being able to be as successful as they and others think they should be. With fast-growth megachurch success stories, pastors may think that something is fundamentally wrong if their congregation hasn't reached a thousand members or is not growing by leaps and bounds. They can have serious doubts when the needs are great, the finances are skimpy, and the ministry seems to limp along with little reserve or resource.

■ Pressure to Perform

This pressure to perform is taking its toll. Listen to what clergy and their families say about the challenge of shepherding God's flock.

"No other vocation is required to represent God to a generation of sophisticated, materialistic, entertainment-prone audiences who need to be told truths that they don't want to hear and be grateful enough for the telling to put money in the collection tray." That was Don's opening statement to me. He was struggling with the bitterness caused by a number of key families leaving the church. They never talked to him about their concerns; they just left! They did, however, complain to everyone else that he had not done a good enough job with Sunday school and visitation.

"What do they expect of me? I can't do everything!" Don protested.

Clergy, like Don, have all these hats that they need to wear in order to do well. When questioned, congregants often say they don't expect the pastor to do everything. But each has his or her personal area of concern. As my brother-in-law says, "Everyone wants a piece of the preacher." Multiply that by one hundred people and you have an average church in America. Don added: "They expect me to preach well, manage the church perfectly, know their names and the names of all their kids and grandkids, visit them when they're sick, and of course stay morally above reproach and never be grumpy when they call me at midnight. How can any one person do all that?"

Expectations of clergy are possibly greater than any other profession. According to pollster George Barna, 73 percent of surveyed Americans expect clergy to live up to higher standards of moral and ethical conduct than they expect of self or others.[1] Even the president of the United States is not expected to live up to a pastor's code of behavior!

■ Performance Is All That Counts

Coupled with high expectations is the premium we place on successful performance and the consequences of failure. Consider Rick's story. He successfully pastored a six-hundred-member denominational church in the suburbs of a large metropolitan area, but unresolved marital problems prompted him to resign. Months later he still feels deeply wounded by the experience.

"Only one person called me and checked on me to see how I was doing. I poured my life into that church and the men I mentored. You would think that they would have shown some care and concern. I can accept the fact that my problematic marriage caused me to fail. What I can't resolve is how the only thing that seemed to count with them [the congregation] was how well I performed. They didn't care about me. They only cared about what I could do for them."

When shepherds disappoint their flocks, there is often a backlash from congregants. A frequently heard phrase from pastors is "sheep bite." People don't expect clergy to have feet of clay. They are our heroes. We think they are the greatest when they share a particularly touching sermon. It's almost like they are one step closer to God than the rest of us. So when expectations aren't met, when they disappoint us, or when they fail, we react. Our heroes become villains. They fall off the pedestal, and we find ourselves despising them. We have great difficulty reconciling their human frailty with our expectations.

■ Fears of Failure and Inadequacy

Rick always feared that he would fail and thus disqualify himself from ministry. Many pastors can identify with that fear. When crowds are not easily pleased or personal and organizational problems arise, clergy feel inadequate and fear failure. Ninety percent of surveyed clergy report they were inadequately trained to cope with the high demands of ministry, and 50 percent feel unable to meet the current needs of the job.[2] When faced with the fears and the pressures of ministry, many become depressed (80 percent of pastors are discouraged or are dealing with depression[3]) or retreat into unhealthy coping behaviors. For example, 37 percent of surveyed pastors admit to having been involved in inappropriate sexual behavior with someone in the church.[4]

Doug, a tall, good-looking man of sixty, was known for his booming voice and eloquent sermons. His gambling problem began innocently on a cruise. He bet a few dollars here and there and surprisingly won a jackpot. Upon returning home he took the risky step of visiting a casino on an Indian reservation just outside of Phoenix. Now he's worried. "I have been spending upwards of a hundred a week on slot machines. I just sit in front of the machine putting dollars in until I lose it all. I know I shouldn't be doing this. But for some strange reason it feels good."

Doug has been coping with ministry pressures in all the wrong ways. He lost an associate six months ago and has been working harder than ever. He only went on the cruise because his grown children gave him and his wife the trip for an anniversary present. He doesn't sleep well and has become less emotionally involved with her, the kids, and the grandkids. His wife doesn't know about the gambling but wonders where he goes after lunch. Doug has never shared his fears and concerns with his wife.

"It just makes her upset when I confide in her about ministry problems. She doesn't know that some of the church elders are unhappy with how things are going. I don't know who to talk to. I never have shared much with anyone. Everyone knows you can't go talking to members of your congregation about what you're really thinking."

Doug's long-standing habit of not sharing inner thoughts or feelings has contributed to his depression and gambling problem. Oftentimes, risky behavior, instead of transparency, becomes the welcome relief for numbed feelings, burnout, and depression caused by prolonged stress.

Most of us don't deal well with stress. Studies indicate that when faced with ongoing stress, many resort to escapist behaviors such as procrastination, excessive sleeping, binge drinking, and overeating. Others become worried and sleepless and experience panic attacks. Pastors are no exception.

I often challenge my friend Gary about how busy he is and ask him if he is taking care of himself—especially when he seems troubled and impatient. Sometimes I think he lives on the edge of burnout. Leaders like Gary often speak casually about burnout, not realizing it may be the number one malady in ministry.

■ Finish Well or Burn Out?

Rob, the pastor of a thriving church, is ready to give it all up and leave the ministry. He says, "I just can't hold it together anymore. I have a hard time praying and feeling passionate about preaching or ministering to others." He feels overwhelmed and anxious most of the time, and he is not sleeping well. He finds concentrating on different tasks difficult and dreads answering phone calls. His wife complains that he is easily irritated with her and the children. He is upset with his board of elders and the way they keep pressuring him to change. Even though he founded the church, the elders complain about his administrative style, and they want to be more directly involved in running the church. To complicate matters, Rob's wife doesn't voice her concerns about how he is doing. She struggles with her own increased pressures and responsibilities in ministry and fears his reaction.

All too often the substantial external pressures of ministry exceed one's internal coping resources. When this happens, as it did in Rob's case—and Doug's—a state of fatigue and frustration can result. We call this *burnout*. Herbert Freudenberger says in *When Helping Starts to Hurt* that burnout is "a state of fatigue or frustration brought about by devotion to a cause, a way of life, or relationship that failed to produce the expected reward."[5]

Rob does not realize that he is experiencing burnout. Burnout and depression are endemic in ministry because of the high expectation to perform and the deep desire to take care of others. People expect more of clergy, and clergy expect more of themselves. Scripture, as well, sets a higher standard (see, e.g., 1 Tim. 3–4; James 3:1). Rob was always there for everyone—his staff, the church members, and the local ministerial association. He tried to be all things to all people all the time.

Rob came to a crisis point before he reached out for help. Doug called me because he knew that mindlessly cranking dollars into slot machines signaled something deeply wrong. Neither realized that burnout was the underlying issue.

After a few counseling sessions and a confession to his wife, Doug's desire to gamble left. Both Rob and Doug, however, needed to make major changes in how they lived out their calling and how they managed their calendar, commitments, and relationships. Both have since learned how to share more intimately with their wives and especially others. They have experienced the balance that comes from opening their lives to input and support from trusted others. They are pursuing shared lives that help them keep healthy and fruitful in fulfilling their call.

■ Avoiding Burnout

So what does it take to avoid burnout and depression, to "not become weary in doing good" (Gal. 6:9)? Is it just a matter of knowing more about the interior of your life? No. One also needs to understand how to lead a life that is conducive to pastoral excellence and finishing well. A minister of the gospel must understand the serious necessity of caring for oneself in a manner that promotes health and longevity. Herein is the major problem: Most clergy are caretakers of others, the church, the congregants, the community, their staff, and their own families, but rarely are they good caretakers of self. To finish well, one must embrace key principles and practices that are helpful in avoiding burnout, such as:

1. *Focus on God's direction and expectations, not on those of others* (1 Sam. 16:7). Don't try to be all things to all people all the time. It is easy to put too much importance on pleasing others and not enough on pleasing God. Attempting to be popular and well liked by your congregants is a snare (Prov. 29:25) that will cause you to compromise for fear of offending them, thus creating an enormous burden.

Jesus modeled this, as John tells us: "Jesus would not entrust himself to them, for he knew all men" (John 2:24). In other words, Jesus gave himself *for* the people, but he did not give himself *to* the people. Jesus came to save us and to serve us, but he was not codependent!

2. *Embrace your strengths and find support for your weaknesses* (Exod. 18:17–18; Eph. 4:11–13). Just as Moses could not bear up under the load of judging the entire nation and needed help, so did Gary. He was doing everything—preaching, teaching, traveling, writing, and trying to manage a very large church staff. He had never taken time to find out what he was mainly called and gifted to do.

Finally, Daryl and Harold, two of his close friends, and I told him that he needed to make a change, to let go of trying to do everything and control everything and let someone else more adept in administration run the day-to-day affairs of the church. We also told him that he wasn't doing a very effective job of management. Ouch! I know that was hard for him to accept.

For a while, I think Gary wondered if we were for him or against him, but we remained convinced that he would burn out and the church would falter if he wasn't able to focus more on using his strengths and let someone else stand alongside him in his weak areas. We also remained committed to him. He is our friend. We care about him.

When Gary finally let go, he was able to identify and focus on his strengths, find support for his weaker areas, and delegate those responsibilities. His stress lessened considerably, and he is now thankful for the change.

3. *Balance your lifestyle and establish good boundaries.* A balanced life contains scheduled time for work, play, family, friends, prayer, and personal care. Ministry leaders often overemphasize work and spend little time playing or socializing with family and friends. Appropriately balancing one's lifestyle requires clearly defined boundaries.

One of Rob's major problems is that he lacks healthy boundaries. Firm boundaries must be in place in the following areas in order to prevent burnout:

- *Separate office from home.* Rob, like many ministers, keeps an office at home. When home also becomes a workplace, you never truly rest from your labor, which leads to increased stress.

- *If married to another minister, keep ministry talk at the office.* Rob's wife is head of a growing women's ministry at the church. They frequently "talk shop" and rarely separate their personal life from their ministry life. The result is a weakened marriage and more stress.

- *Separate study time from personal devotions and prayer* (Isa. 40:31). Doug falls into the common trap of not cultivating a personal prayer time that addresses his own need to be in the presence of the Lord. His prayer time increasingly centers on praying for others and preparing for the Sunday and Wednesday messages. He has lost touch with God's word to him on a personal level addressing his own life.

- *Do not make social time or playtime one more opportunity for ministering to others* (Mark 6:31). Rob has a consistent pattern of utilizing scheduled playtime for ministering to others. He feels guilty when he takes time for himself. "When I relax, I feel guilty" is a common refrain of many ministry leaders. They tend to burn out because they are too busy doing God's work and unrealistically squeeze more into a schedule than is reasonable. A balance of work and play allows God to refresh and renew you during the times away from ministry pressures.

- *Schedule weekly time off, quarterly timeouts, and annual vacations.* Stress experts recommend weekly, quarterly, and annual respites. Finishing well, which means completing one's ministry in grace, requires scheduled periods of refreshment and reflection away from ministry expectations and pressures—discipline that Doug had never considered because there was always "so much to do."

4. *Be health conscious* (1 Cor. 3:16–17). Burnout is due not only to erosion of spirit but also to physical exhaustion. A healthy body wards off negative stress and increases your ability to deal with pressure. Rob's twenty extra pounds, lack

of exercise, and poor eating habits contribute to his burnout. Hundreds of how-to books on exercise, nutrition, and care for the body are available. Usually our problem is not a lack of information but lack of commitment to a disciplined program of health.

5. *Do not allow secrets from the past, hidden problems, and sin to remain unconfessed* (Prov. 28:13; James 5:16). Secret areas of pain, problems, or sin will cause a significant increase in stress. Secrets always carry the stress of shame until confessed. Rob confessed that he had visited Internet porn sites. Relief and accountability came with the sharing. Doug even felt more depressed when he kept his gambling addiction to himself, like the psalmist who wrote, "There was a time when I wouldn't admit what a sinner I was. But my dishonesty made me miserable and filled my days with frustration" (Ps. 32:3 TLB). Confession to another and embracing a plan of change will reduce stress even if the problem or sin is not yet conquered.

■ Possibly the Most Important Tip of All

In times of stress and difficulty, call upon the Lord and your brothers in Christ (Pss. 25:18; 106:44; Prov. 18:24; 27:10). Many of the things Rob and Doug changed in their lives were things they already knew to do! They didn't just need more teaching and more information! They needed a transparent, honest, and accountable relationship. They never would have had to see a therapist (me, Al!) if they had the support of solid peer friendships in which they could hear the truth. People who burn out live isolated, unhealthy lives, making them more prone to failure.

Gary is fond of saying, "Al saved my life." The truth of the matter is that Gary's commitment to relationship saved his life—and mine. I'll never forget the day he was jogging past my house and decided to stop in for a moment to see how I was doing. It was a God thing. I was struggling with whether I should leave my position as head of a Christian counseling clinic and go to work for an acquaintance as national director of an inpatient alcohol and drug abuse system. I had been pressured to "put out a fleece" in order to make the decision. I was agonizing over what to do when Gary showed up.

"Don't you know you can get 'fleeced' by putting out a fleece?" he proclaimed. The cloud lifted and clarity came. I didn't take the job and have been glad ever since that I didn't. Gary was God's gift in the moment, a friend in time of need.

■ Hurting Families

Pastors aren't the only ones who need care, concern, and support. Their families are another crucial area of concern. Often neglected and rarely understood or appreciated, many of them are hurting.

"I don't like Christians after what I've seen 'good Christians' do to my dad!" exclaimed Daryl's daughter.

Daryl founded and pastored an independent church in the Southwest. Two staff members unexpectedly left and started their own church, drawing people away. Once a thriving independent work of more than 700 people, the church now averages 300 to 350 attendees a weekend. Daryl feels deeply betrayed and discouraged. "I never expected this," he said. "It is hard to see everything you have worked for decline so quickly. It hurts a lot. And it really bothers me to think my kids have this jaundiced view of ministry and Christians."

Possibly the greatest disappointment for clergy is the sad and painful status of their families. Eighty percent of those surveyed believe that pastoral ministry has affected their families negatively, and 33 percent say that being in ministry is an outright hazard to their family.[6] When spouses of clergy were surveyed, 84 percent reported being discouraged and in depression.[7] George Barna's research confirms the dire effects of ministry on families, with 49 percent of surveyed individuals contending that their family life has suffered significantly as a result of the pressures and demand of their ministry.[8]

Daryl's daughter is married and has a family of her own. Her husband, Greg, helped out with the youth program at the church and is considering going into full-time vocational ministry. She said, "I told Greg that I couldn't do it. I could never be a pastor's wife. I don't know how my mother endured all those years of pain. I still have trouble going to church on Sunday and sitting through a sermon. In truth, the main reason I go is for Greg and the kids' sake."

Daryl's wife, Janice, also didn't handle the pain well. After the second church split, she became so depressed that Daryl asked a physician friend to prescribe her medication. They kept it a secret, because in their circle of ministry, taking medication for depression is seen as not having enough faith in God.

My heart cries for the family members. They feel the pain as acutely as the point man, the leader, but they have even less say about what happens in their lives—less control and fewer resources to bring about constructive change in their local church. They also often don't have close friends. After all, in whom can you confide when the pastor is your husband or father and you don't want to cause more problems?

■ Another Typical Story

Melody is growing more numb and shut down by the day. Her husband lost his church, and she, a preacher's kid, can't take the pain.

"I hate church people. I hate what they did to my dad. He was never the same after losing the church, and now I hate what they are doing to Ron and me. They are so mean."

Melody is good at helping others with their pain but unable to handle her own. She has never had a close friend with whom she can cry and pray about the losses and disappointments in her life, especially the ones that come with ministry and people problems. She has never learned to share her burdens with others, and she certainly couldn't share with her mom and dad, who were also in crisis. So she silently suffered and remains bitter about her father's legacy of faithful service to God and others.

■ The Real Problem

Each of these ministers and their families share a common problem: When faced with conflict, a crisis, or even normal life difficulties, they have no one to talk to. Nobody is there to provide safe and helpful support. Seventy percent of those in ministry report they do not have someone they consider a close friend,[9] someone who could serve as a confidant during times of difficulty. Most clergy report that at one time or another they confided in a member of the congregation or a church leader with disastrous results.

As leaders we all are afraid of being too transparent and possibly rejected for not measuring up. We also fear letting people down if they really knew how much we struggled with life like they do. What would they think of us then? Dare we admit that we too are imperfect and need to keep changing, that our goal in life is Christlikeness, just like that of the people we serve?

When Gary was feeling stressed and harried, the last thing he wanted was more pressure, especially pressure that required change. Yet change was what was needed. God could only grow the ministry as far as Gary was willing to grow personally. Gary's willingness to develop friendships and to invite me and other men into his life was pivotal to supporting his needed change.

When problems arise we leaders often go to great lengths to preserve the ministry instead of doing whatever it takes to change personally. In times of difficulty we need words of encouragement and safe, supportive, yet honest friends. We need friends who can help us hold steady and help with the pain and discouragement as well as support what needs to be changed. We need friends who will "love at all times" (Prov. 17:17) and who "stick closer than a brother" (Prov. 18:24).

Isolation and lack of an understanding friend deprive us of the God-given outlet for stress in our lives and can lead to burnout and even failure in ministry. We need to overcome our fears and isolation through healthy peer friendships. We need to develop friendships with others in ministry and go out of our way to maintain them. We need each other.

The Perfect Church

Church work confuses relational worlds more than any other profession.

—Bill Hybels

I (Gary) had a church staff problem.

So what else is new.

One of our leaders came into my office wanting to talk to me about some things. His red eyes betrayed the depth of his distress. Elements of his work at our church, specifically in the way I was "supervising" the staff, were causing him a lot of pain.

Not giving me any specifics (So what else is new?), he told me he wanted me to schedule a two-hour block of time for him to discuss his concerns. We needed that much time, he assured me, and because he had a high level of anxiety about the meeting, he informed me he needed someone there to support him—his wife. She had issues too, he told me.

I agreed to the meeting, with someone else there to help us listen to one another and to talk us through the issues, but not

41

his spouse. We met for more than two hours, and with the help of an objective third party, we began a journey of resolution.

Although awkward and potentially explosive meetings like this occur with regrettable frequency in local churches of every size and variety, they virtually *never* happen in the business world. I mean, really, have you ever heard of a bank employee, a schoolteacher, or a steel worker telling his boss that he needed to talk about problems at work but that he wanted to bring his wife?

Only in the church!

■ But God Told Me . . .

Here are a few things I've heard, every one of them a real church situation:

- An employee of the church complains to his supervisor that a relative of his, who is also working for the church, is not getting paid enough. (In the business community, most companies have strict policies and guidelines for family members who work for the company.)
- A church custodian is consistently late for work, and when told he must punch in on time or risk losing his job, he objects, "But this is a church!"
- An associate minister has to be terminated for moral failure, and members of the staff complain that the leadership of the church should have forgiven him and let him keep his job.
- A staff person resigns. Within a week, her husband, a board member, calls to arrange a meeting with the senior pastor "to discuss" the situation.
- The youth pastor's wife's sister is the secretary to the senior pastor. Her mother is the church receptionist.
- A large church has to ask a prominent staff leader to resign. Other staff members protest, rallying "the paying customers." They make it clear that the dismissed pas-

tor was the only reason they go to the church. And "the company" breaks up.

- A worship leader will not cooperate with the senior pastor because she answers to a Higher Power. You know, it's the "God told me" thing. (If you don't work in a church, try this one on your boss—or on your commanding officer if you're in the marines.)

Only in the church!

Years ago the worship minister on my staff told me that someday he was going to write a book, *My Pastor, My Boss, My Friend.* He was joking, of course, but it was his way of saying that my multifaceted relationship with him was thoroughly confusing. I *was* his pastor; we had brought him on staff right out of our congregation. So I cared about him, wanted the best for him, forgave him. I was his friend too; we traveled in ministry together, and we did things together with our wives. But I was also his boss; I had expectations for him as an employee of our ministry, which meant I had to tell him what to do. And, God have mercy, sometimes I had to correct him.

Only in the church!

Did you hear about the guy stranded alone for thirty years on a little island? He finally waved down a ship, and when the first mate came ashore in a lifeboat, he saw three huts at the edge of the jungle. "What are those huts?" he asked. "Well," the castaway replied, pointing to the first hut, "That one is where I live, and," pointing to the third, "that's where I go to church."

"What about the middle hut?" the first mate asked.

"Oh," the man said, "that's where I used to go to church."

■ Church Culture

What we're really talking about here is church culture—the uniquely complex theological and sociological elements of church life. Think about it: a business is not an army is not a family. But the church is all of these things at the same time.

Like a family, everyone in the church is loved and accepted equally, regardless of competence or skill—at least everyone is supposed to be. In a family, however, it doesn't matter if someone is just learning to play the piano. You love that person and listen anyway, and you praise him or her.

As a business, though, the church has organizational structure, employees, and a bottom line. You can put your head in the sand and make believe that it doesn't matter, but if a church has bad music, it affects the bottom line. And somebody is going to have to replace that novice musician who just happens to be the daughter of the head elder.

There is a fundamental incompatibility between family and business, which is why so many family businesses (and churches?) are notoriously dysfunctional. But there's more. Complicating matters further, the church is also an army, in which there must be absolute submission and obedience to authority, in which people are called to lay down their lives, and in which, because there's a real enemy, people die. Paul alludes to this in his famous statement in Ephesians 6:12, "Our struggle is not against flesh and blood." Paul's use of the term "struggle" has gladiator overtones. Eugene Peterson brings this out well in *The Message,* his contemporary translation of the Bible: "This is for keeps, a life-or-death fight to the finish against the Devil and all his angels."

■ A Reason to Die

I was told the true story of the youngest captain in the Australian army in World War II. As he was leading a hundred or so men in an advance on an enemy position, his company encountered an unmarked minefield directly between them and their objective. The young captain told his men, "We have orders to advance to that position on the other side of this minefield. I need five men to volunteer to run through that field and detonate the mines so we can advance."

With little hesitation, *everyone* in the company raised his hand to volunteer for an assignment that would end his life.

"You . . . and you," sputtered the captain, ". . . and you . . . and you . . . and you."

Five young men died, and the company advanced.

Never in the church! At least not in places in the world where people aren't desperate for God.

■ Systems

Unhealthy, dysfunctional church culture is the first of three elements of what Al and I have referred to as the unholy trinity of unhealthy church life. The second is the neglect of systems. Let us explain. I (Gary) have the gift of gab. In more religious terms, I really do have the anointing to preach and teach the Bible, and thousands of people come to hear me talk. And that could give me the illusion that I'm more right than just about everybody else.

Well, people come with problems, and our calling as a local church is not just to get people through the door of heaven, but to turn irreligious people into fully devoted followers of Jesus Christ. And how do you do that? You have to have a plan, a structure, and a system. Imagine a university without a curriculum, a history course with no tests, an unassembled bike without step-by-step assembly instructions, or a baseball game without rules, foul lines, or a beginning and an ending.

I can imagine, though, a church without any plan to do much more than a one-hour service on Sunday mornings. And some churches barely have plans for that. Taking it a step further, if a church does have a plan, somebody has to lead a team of people to make the plan happen and to hold them accountable if it doesn't. Naturally, the more people in the church, the more sophisticated the plan becomes. Ask Moses, who was overwhelmed with pastoral counseling. His father-in-law, Jethro, saved his life with a plan and a structure to carry out that plan (see Exod. 18:13–26).

Really, it's very simple, but I can't tell you how many times church culture screams, "You can't run this place like a business!"[1] What people mean, of course, is that somehow organization and spirituality are incompatible, even though one of the gifts of the Spirit in Romans 12 is administration.

Certainly the church is not *primarily* a business, meaning it doesn't exist to make money, and the business of the church must serve the mission of the church, never the other way around; but implementing good, sound business practices in the leadership of the local church is necessary. "If the ax is dull and its edge unsharpened," the ancient text tells us, "more strength is needed but skill will bring success" (Eccles. 10:10).

■ The Perfect Church

"There is no such thing as a perfect church."

How many times have we heard that one? Well, it's true—sort of. In the New Testament meaning of the term *perfect*, however, a "perfect church," it seems, should be attainable, for the Greek term translated "perfect" does not mean "flawless." So very different from the English word *perfect* often used to translate it, the Greek word *telieos* means "full, whole, complete, mature." Consider these notable places where the term in one of its several forms is used in the New Testament (I have italicized the English translation of the Greek term):

- "When he had received the drink, Jesus said, *'It is finished.'* With that, he bowed his head and gave up his spirit" (John 19:30). Jesus said, "It has been made *perfect.*"
- "By one sacrifice he has *made perfect* forever those who are being made holy" (Heb. 10:14).
- "Perseverance must finish its work so that you may be *mature and complete,* not lacking anything" (James 1:4).
- It was he who gave some to be apostles, some to be prophets, some to be evangelists, and some to be pastors and teachers, to prepare God's people for works of service, so that the body of Christ may be built up until we all reach unity in the faith and in the knowledge of the

Son of God and become *mature,* attaining to the whole measure of the fullness of Christ (Eph. 4:11–13).

Obviously, "perfect" in the context of these passages is more than a remote possibility. Without a doubt, God wants his church to be whole, mature, fully formed, or, to use a popular term, *healthy.* Al and I contend that for a local church to be perfect—that is, healthy—three things need to happen, and probably in the following order:

1. The pastor/leader must be healthy.
2. The culture must be healthy.
3. The leadership and management systems must be healthy.

These three elements, of course, are mutually inclusive, and each is important. For example, a church can have blue ribbon management systems, but if the pastor has an affair with his secretary, you can kiss that church good-bye. Or, at best, you can put it into recovery for a few years. Instead of fully formed, many churches are deformed. In one of the lesser-known verses in the Bible, Paul scolds the Corinthians for tolerating such an unhealthy church: "In the following directives I have no praise for you, for your meetings do more harm than good" (1 Cor. 11:17).

Ouch! Can you imagine God saying that about your church? "Your meetings do more harm than good." Sounds like unchurched people might actually have a biblical reason for not going to church!

So what makes a church "perfect"? Let's look at these three elements in reverse order. First, here are some of the elements of a healthy church culture:

- a culture that manages and resolves conflict
- an environment of love, acceptance, and forgiveness
- a place where people are encouraged to learn from their mistakes

■ Conflict in the Church

I (Al) want to talk about the role of conflict in church culture and especially in the life of the leader who sets the culture. Perhaps the single greatest characteristic of healthy church culture is its ability to appropriately—biblically—manage and resolve conflict. Conflict is a normal and natural part of life within both the church and the secular world. Churches are full of conflict because churches are made up of people—needy, hurting, struggling people. And wherever people congregate, conflict and problems arise.

Many don't expect there to be conflict in the church even though conflict is an inescapable element of human life, even good Christian human life! Conflict will happen! It happens frequently in the church, because church life is all about people and relationships—with God and one another. Most congregants have high expectations of their church. When communication breaks down, when expectations aren't met and needs conflict, people in the church expect the pastor to "fix it" or prevent it. "He should be able to handle conflict well and help resolve everyone else's conflicts," one church member asserted. "After all, if you can't or aren't supposed to go to court, then who can you turn to if not the church?"

In reality, one's ability to effectively resolve conflict greatly affects the ability to lead and sets the tone for dealing with conflict in the life of the church. Unresolved and mismanaged conflict contributes substantially to burnout and failure. Gary and I understand this well. We have witnessed the damage unresolved and mismanaged conflict has caused in the lives of ministry friends and in the ministries they lead.

■ Our Attitude toward Conflict

Our attitude toward conflict shapes how we handle it. Conflict can be healthy in relationships. The love, care, and concern we need should be balanced with challenge, sacrifice, and change. "As iron sharpens iron," the Scripture says, "so one man sharpens another" (Prov. 27:17). An ax head produces sparks when sharpened against a grinding wheel. A healthy church conflict can also sharpen rough edges despite the sparks that fly. Rightly managed conflict makes us stretch beyond our self-centeredness, requiring us to push past our emotional comfort levels and learn how to lead better. Conflict doesn't have to be negative or hurt people. Often, though, conflict between members and the pastor or his staff has disastrous results. Nobody wins, everyone loses.

■ High Levels of Mismanaged Conflict

Conflict is hard for all of us to deal with. Very few people are skilled in handling conflict biblically and effectively. Many congregants mismanage conflict and do a poor job of approaching church leaders with issues of conflict. They typically avoid conflict, complain about problems without offering solutions, and may even leave the pastor a "nasty note" as they leave the church. Or they attack first, leave later. Others may stay and keep the fire of conflict burning until the pastor, overwhelmed by the relentless conflict, leaves.

Sadly, most clergy are also not well trained in how to handle conflict even though they regularly face significant levels of interpersonal conflict. A Fuller Institute study reported that 40 percent of ministers surveyed had a serious conflict with a parishioner at least once a month. That's a lot of conflict! And 75 percent reported a significant stress-related crisis at least once a month in their ministry.[2] *Leadership* magazine found that 25 percent of those asked said they had been fired or forced to resign, normally by a faction of people that numbered fewer than ten.[3]

■ Avoiding Conflict

If conflict in the church is so potentially disastrous, what can be done to make it better? First of all, don't avoid it. Being intimidated by it or pretending it is not there will only increase the potential for damage.

"There's always someone upset about something," shared Ray. "I try to avoid the complainers. If someone wants to talk to me, I tell him to speak to my associate, Dan. I can't expose myself to everyone's opinion." Ray's style of dealing with conflict is obviously one of avoidance. The pressures and demands of the job are great, and he tries to avoid conflict so that he won't have more pressures and problems. Avoidance is a common way of dealing with the inevitable conflicts of ministry, but it is not the best one. When conflict is avoided, nothing gets resolved. The pressure and problems don't go away. Instead, they build up like water behind a dam until, under pressure, the dam breaks, and everyone in its shadow is drowned in a flood of emotion, hostility, and pain.

Ray's wife is increasingly frustrated with his pattern of withdrawal and avoidance. At her breaking point, she confessed to me, "Ray is so hard to pin down. He won't talk to me. Whenever there is a problem with one of the kids or the finances, he just expects me to handle it without his help. Or he quickly tells me what he thinks and then says he has to go. I'm tired of having to go it alone. I can't keep doing this."

Ray's avoidance pattern not only results in growing exasperation at home but also a troubling cycle of growth and loss at the church. Each time the church gets beyond 250 to 300 attendees, someone becomes disgruntled enough to lead a minor revolt, and people leave the church. After the third exodus, Ray's elders forced him to seek counsel. He shared his view of conflict: "I don't like conflict. I never have and probably never will. My mom and dad fought all the time, and I remember going into my room and turning the music up so I didn't have to hear."

■ Old Patterns That Need to Change

We learn how to resolve conflict in our families of origin and then usually reenact with others what we learned while growing up. For example, in my (Al's) family, conflict was usually met with irritation and, if not easily resolved, could provoke explosive anger. Later on amends might be made for the anger, but the issue we fought over would rarely be discussed again or resolved. In the early years of my marriage, this was how I dealt with conflict with my wife and others. Our relationship was heading for major problems until Susan and I learned how to resolve conflict God's way.

All of us learn patterns of managing conflict from our family past. Ray's unhealthy pattern was formed in the incubation of his family life and is being lived out in the way he pastors (or avoids) the people in his church. He must change if he wants to keep his church and family intact.

■ Winning through Anger and Intimidation?

Henry's style is also counterproductive. "I'm here because my elders and my wife think I have a problem with anger," Henry declared in a counseling session. "I'm just tired of people causing trouble and getting away with it. When I confront them on their sin, my elders say I am too hostile. You would be too if you had to put up with some of the dumb things supposedly smart people do."

I (Al) believe our culture is full of angry people. We have angry spouses, random shootings, and gang wars. But anger isn't just out there; we have anger in the pulpit and pew too.

A major cause of conflict in the church is not just theological difference but unresolved anger, something the apostle Paul calls "the dividing wall of hostility" (Eph. 2:14). Difference doesn't divide us. Angry conflict over our differences is what leaves us feeling helpless and alone; unresolved anger prevents unity and destroys cooperation. It leads to "win" styles of resolving conflict, wherein the confronter firmly believes, "I'm right, and they're wrong! And I'm going to show them how wrong they are."

This is where a good friend can help. One evening around eight o'clock I received a phone call from Gary. He was particularly upset and angry with a staff member who was causing undue stress in the organization and blaming everyone else, including him.

"Who is going to correct him?" Gary demanded. "He's driving me and everyone crazy! I can't take it anymore. He ought to be fired! He's the one causing all the trouble."

I listened to Gary patiently, hearing his frustration and hurt, but I also challenged him. "Take the high road. You're the leader. Show him how a man of God handles conflict. Follow the leading of God, not the demands of your emotions."

At the end of our lengthy phone call, Gary said softly, "Thanks, friend." Gary surrendered his feelings to God and made every effort to resolve the conflict in a godly manner. As leaders we must make a commitment to resolve conflict in an environment of honesty and a spirit of grace.

■ Human Anger Doesn't Accomplish God's Purposes

When people are angry they experience a feeling of greater power or potency than when they aren't angry. No wonder angry people often feel very little desire to change or to control their anger. The only other emotion people are less likely to want to change is joy! Anger, for many, becomes the substitute empowerment for dealing with the ongoing feelings of frustration, challenge, and stress.

One of the major cluster symptoms of burnout is increased frustration, impatience, and anger. Henry had to change how he viewed himself and others. He also had to learn how to appropriately resolve his own anger and conflict with others.

"I didn't know that I was stressed out and angry. I used to think I was just 'bothered' or 'upset' at someone, when in reality I was experiencing anger. In my church circles, anger is viewed as an undesirable emotion. No one dare admit they are angry! I guess it was easier for me to believe it was my job to set them right instead of dealing with my own anger and stress. Now, when necessary, I speak the truth in love and openly share that I have problems dealing with my own anger."

■ Doing It Right

There are many models and tools for resolving conflict in a biblical and Christ-honoring manner. Peacemaker Ministries in Billings, Montana (406-256-1583; www.peacemakerministries .org), does a great job of coaching individual Christians and churches on how to resolve conflict. Perhaps the most necessary, yet difficult, part of resolving conflict is ensuring that you maintain control of yourself. Proverbs 16:32 says, "Better a patient man than a warrior, a man who controls his temper than one who takes a city." The good news is that Jesus will not leave you helpless! He has given us his Holy Spirit to empower us, to give us some measure of victory over our carnal nature in this life.

Be sure you admit to your feelings of anger, fear, and offense. People justify their thoughts, feelings, and actions when they are angry. Anger is an emotion that does not easily yield to personal responsibility. Instead, we want to blame others for making us angry. Be quick to discuss with a trusted friend your feelings and your thoughts and your need to resolve your anger before acting. The transparency will help you better understand yourself, the problem, and what God wants you to do as well as provide needed accountability. It will also help you keep your church healthy. "Confess your sins to each other," James writes, "and pray for each other so that you may be healed" (James 5:16).

■ Healthy Systems

In the widely read *Natural Church Development: A Guide to Eight Essential Qualities of Healthy Churches,* Christian A. Schwarz notes that the development of organizational systems was "by far the most controversial of the eight quality characteristics." Spiritually oriented people, he observes, "tend to be skeptical of structures, deeming them unspiritual."[4] What Al and I call "systems," Christian Schwarz refers to as "functional structures." The larger question is this: What makes for healthy systems and what might be some "dysfunctional structures"? We have no simple definition, but healthy systems would include *clearly defined* things like:

- a written statement of mission, with goals and strategies to achieve that mission
- a list of core values to which everyone in leadership agrees and to which he or she makes a personal commitment
- the role of the governing board and its relationship to the senior pastor (and staff in larger churches)
- differences in the roles of governance, leadership, and administration
- an understanding of how decisions are made
- job descriptions for staff and/or volunteer leaders
- an annual audit
- a policy manual for staff and volunteers
- written guidelines for conflict resolution and a commitment by everyone in leadership to abide by those guidelines
- a fair and equitable system for compensating the pastor (and staff in larger churches)

Notice that above the bullet points we emphasized the phrase "clearly defined." By this we mean hammered out—sometimes word by word, by the people designing and leading the systems—and written down. Simply stated, what people don't understand, they misunderstand. Many fine Christian leaders, though, either object to or resist writing things down. Perhaps they think it sounds like legalism. Or maybe they just don't know how to do it. Or could it be that it's just too much work?

My former senior associate pastor—and still good friend— Bob Blayter, a lover of systems, has a classic response for people who are reluctant to write things down: *the Bible*. Yes, the Bible is a fair indicator of how God himself thinks it is important to write things down! Imagine, sometimes we Christians can hardly get along *with* the Bible. What would it be like if our faith rested only on the subjective experiences passed on from one generation to the next?

■ Healthy Leaders

What makes for healthy leaders? Gary and I believe that a well-lived pastoral life is an ongoing journey. It is one characterized by excitement, adventure, and success as well as challenge, problems, and struggles. Healthy leaders need a balanced approach to building their ministries, an approach that embraces both practical and theological tools to help them with the daily demands of ministry and with their long-term development as leaders.

We all realize that leaders need continual study in how to read and embrace biblical texts in ways that provide answers for themselves, their congregations, and the communities in which they serve. We also believe that leaders need significant relationships that support personal health, long-term viability, and essential values. When one reviews the challenges of pastoral ministry today, it is clear that pastors need safe places, safe times, and safe people in which to confront and overcome those challenges. We believe a healthy pastoral life encompasses more than knowledge and skill; it requires embracing key core ministry values, some of which we have discussed.

To summarize, here are some of our thoughts about what it means to be a healthy leader:

- personal authenticity and openness (a church culture issue), not closed and crafty
- confidence in whom God has made you to be and the calling of God on your life, not fearful and controlling (a church systems issue)
- an investment of time in your personal relationship with God

- a serious investment of time in your relationships with others

In the next several chapters, we will develop a couple of the key elements of healthy spiritual leadership, ones that we believe provide the foundation for meeting the challenges of a well-lived pastoral life. Those elements are:

- being down to earth, like Jesus
- failing forward
- developing self-awareness
- having friends for life

4

On Being Human

"Where are you staying?"

John 1:38

"What are *you* doing here?"

I (Gary) can't tell you how many times I've heard that from people in my church. Not *at* church. That is where I'm expected to be seen. Inevitably, though, when someone bumps into me at a restaurant or a mall or Wal-Mart, I'm nearly always asked the same question: "What are *you* doing here?" Like it's unusual. Like maybe I should feel guilty for being out in public.

Sometimes church people say the darnedest things—like when I was in a baseball card shop a few years ago and someone from my church walked in. Before I had a chance to say hello, the guy blurted out, "Hey, Gary! So this is what happens to our tithe money." Or the time I was in the garden shop at Kmart. I had been working in the yard and didn't think to change into my Sunday best to pick up a couple bags of ammonium sulfate. In fact, I was, of all things, wearing a T-shirt and shorts! And a woman from church whom I did not recognize (we have a very large congregation) saw me. She put her hand to her mouth in startled surprise and exclaimed (you're not going to believe this), "Pastor Kinnaman, I've never seen your legs before!" I'm sure she meant to say, "I've never seen you in shorts," but you know, when you see the man of God in the garden shop at Kmart, it's such a shock that, well, you just get tongue-tied.

People have even made comments about the novelty of seeing me eat. The best time to visit the zoo, you know, is when they're feeding the animals. Yes, people have actually said things like, "So you eat food like the rest of us?"

Or worse, bathroom comments. Just a few weeks ago a very dear friend, someone I've known for more than fifteen years, passed me in the men's room between services on Sunday morning and remarked, "So you use this room too?" I just had to laugh! It was so incredible! Would you ever under any circumstances be surprised that someone you know is using a restroom?

A few years ago *Leadership Journal* asked pastors to send them true stories of their most outrageous moments in the ministry. One young pastor wrote that he and his wife were not able to have children of their own, so they decided to adopt several kids. An elderly woman in his church, when she found out her pastor's children were adopted, whispered in his ear, "You know, pastor, it's really better when ministers have children that way."

■ Jesus Was Human Too

I've heard this comment a lot too: "Pastor Gary, you are so human." I consider this one a compliment! It makes me feel like I'm really connecting, like somehow people in my congregation have been able to identify with me. Actually, it makes me feel like Jesus. He was so human, so down-to-earth, that people in the religious community could not believe he was the Son of God.

Who among us hasn't said, "We all need to be more like Jesus"? But seldom, if ever, do we mean this: Jesus was fully human, and we need to be more fully human, just like him. No, "being more like Jesus" almost always implies a call to deeper spirituality, higher holiness, and greater power, all of which are certainly valid pursuits for every believer. But for those of us in ministry to be isolated, disconnected from the people we serve, may be a fundamental violation of the spirit of the incarnation: "For we do not have a high priest who is unable to sympathize with our weaknesses, but we have one who has been tempted in every way, just as we are—yet was without sin. Let us then approach the throne of grace with confidence, so that we may receive mercy and find grace to help us in our time of need" (Heb. 4:15–16).

Do we have pastors like this—Christian leaders who are open about their weaknesses and temptation? Role models, not only of what it means to be professionally successful and spiritually strong, but of profound and utter dependence on the grace of God?

Jesus was human too, but for some reason Christians have always seemed to neglect this element of the nature of Christ. This was, in fact, the first "official" heresy in the history of Christianity. In the formative years of the Christian faith, even before the last books of the New Testament had been written, the first apostles were faced with an emerging belief that the humanity of Jesus was secondary to "the Christ" spirit animating his life and ministry.

Known as Gnosticism, or "knowledgism," this view, simply stated, held that relationship and encounter with God occurred on the "higher" level of personal revelation, knowledge, and experience. In elevating the more spiritual elements of the Christian faith, the Gnostics essentially denied the humanity of Christ. To counter this, John wrote his first letter, which begins: "That which was from the beginning, which we have heard, which we have seen with our eyes, which we have looked at and our hands have touched—this we proclaim concerning the Word of life" (1 John 1:1). Jesus the Son of God was not a phantom. Someone who could be seen and touched with the human senses, he was no more or less human than any of us.

John continues: "This is how you can recognize the Spirit of God: Every spirit that acknowledges that Jesus Christ has come in the flesh is from God, but every spirit that does not acknowledge Jesus is not from God. This is the spirit of the antichrist, which you have heard is coming and even now is already in the world" (1 John 4:2–3). We learn from this passage that the humanity of Christ is *essential* to the Christian message. God did not send his Son to deliver us from our humanity, but to deliver our humanity from the curse and bondage of sin. So when people in my church say to me, "Gary, you are so human," I tell them, "I have no idea what else I could be."

Are they implying, perhaps, that other pastors are not human? If that's true, then those leaders are not Christlike, because to be like Jesus is to be fully human, to live in a real world with real people.

- To be helpless: "Come down from the cross, if you are the Son of God!" (Matt. 27:40).
- To doubt: "My God, my God, why have you forsaken me?" (Matt. 27:46).
- To struggle with obedience and the will of God: "Father, if you are willing, take this cup from me; yet not my will, but yours be done" (Luke 22:42).
- To be tempted: "We have one who has been tempted in every way" (Heb. 4:15).
- To suffer and die.
- And through it all, to live by faith in the sufficiency of the grace of God: "My grace is sufficient, for my power is made perfect in weakness" (2 Cor. 12:9).

■ Where Do You Live?

The very first meeting between Jesus and some of his disciples was remarkably earthy, even "unspiritual." John records the moment in the first chapter of his Gospel (vv. 35–39):

The next day John [the Baptist] was there again with two of his disciples. When he saw Jesus passing by, he said, "Look, the Lamb of God!"

When the two disciples heard him say this, they followed Jesus. Turning around, Jesus saw them following and asked, "What do you want?"

What a question! How would you like Jesus to turn to you and make the same offer? How these two disciples responded is extraordinarily ordinary:

They said, "Rabbi" (which means Teacher), "where are you staying?"

"Come," he replied, "and you will see."

The first question these two disciples ask Jesus is not, "Can you tell us about the future?" or even, "Can you tell us more about God?" They simply want to know, "Where are you staying?" or "Where do you live?" Isn't that what everybody wants to know about the preacher? People are curious about where I live and what's in my house. We've even had drive-by "lookings." The reason is obvious: People are far more interested in "where I live"—a metaphor for how I do life—than they are in what I believe.

Jesus gets to the believing part in John 3:16, but his initial encounter with his disciples in John's narrative is relational.

"Where do you live?"

Jesus answers simply, "Come and you will see."

"So they went and saw where he was staying, and spent that day with him." The power point of ministry isn't always the pulpit. It's relationship with people, and that's what gives us a pulpit.

I've found, for example, that as difficult as it was to raise my children, to get them to listen to me, it was flat out impossible to raise the neighbor's children or even my brother's children. Parenting, like pastoring, is rooted in relationship, and we all know that even parenting fails when parents are out of touch—out of relationship—with their children.

"Okay," you might ask, "so what if I'm a Christian leader [a parent?] and I fail?"

What else is new? To err is human. If you "err," then show the people around you, in your family and in your church, how to acknowledge that honestly, how to ask for forgiveness when necessary, and how to appropriate the grace of God. Show them how to "fail forward," as John Maxwell likes to say.

■ Unrealistic Expectations

Simply put, being anything more or less than human is a thoroughly unrealistic expectation, but it's what we Christian leaders face daily. It's at the core of what makes our work so difficult. The ministry is the best job and the worst job, a place of both honor and shame.

Because Christian leadership is so demanding, leaders need leaders. A wealth of social research underscores that pastors and Christian leaders are in big trouble. We face among other things:

- unrealistic expectations
- inadequacy and fear of failure
- unusually high levels of personal conflict
- different standards
- inadequate and dysfunctional church systems
- hurting families
- isolation

Al has already addressed these issues at some length, but I'd like to camp for a while in the jungle of unrealistic expectations, where few of us survive.

■ Not Spiritual Enough

Let's start with spirituality. Here's the unwritten rule: *The pastor must be the most spiritual person in the church.* Tell me, please, where did that come from? Certainly not the Bible. As

I reflect on how the great men and women of God in Scripture were selected and appointed for "full-time ministry," I can't think of a single deserving one. Abraham, who gave his wife to another man and said she was his sister? Moses, the goat keeper? David, another goat keeper? Rahab the prostitute, Ruth the foreigner, Esther the beauty queen, or Mary the commoner? How about Isaiah and Jeremiah or Matthew and Mark? Or Paul! Now there's somebody whose deep spirituality grabbed God's attention!

I'm being sarcastic, of course, because Paul described his years of passionate religion with one little four-letter word: "dung" (Phil. 3:8 KJV). Consider Paul's self-effacing introduction to his Ephesian letter: "Paul, an apostle of Christ Jesus *by the will of God* " (1:1, italics mine). He didn't ask to become an apostle, nor did he make it happen. His place in life was a result of God's calling. I could have begun this chapter much the same way: "Gary, senior pastor of a large church and author *by the will of God.*"

Wait, does that sound self-promoting? I don't think it sounds any more or less self-promoting than when Paul assigned himself the rather lofty title of apostle, but then Paul didn't give himself that title—God did. I have my seminary degrees, and I've been to my share of church success seminars, but looking back, God did that too.

- "May I never boast except in the cross of our Lord Jesus Christ, through which the world has been crucified to me, and I to the world" (Gal. 6:14).
- "If I must boast, I will boast of the things that show my weakness" (2 Cor. 11:30).
- "For who makes you different from anyone else? What do you have that you did not receive? And if you did receive it, why do you boast as though you did not?" (1 Cor. 4:7)

God did not love me or call me because I was spiritual. He called me out of his love, by his grace, for his purposes. I am in full-time Christian ministry because God chose me and, like

Jeremiah, set me apart for himself before I was in my mother's womb (Jer. 1:5). Instead of the above stated unwritten rule, the rule should be: *The pastor/leader must be spiritually minded, but he or she need not be the most spiritual person in the church.*

■ Not Good Enough

Well, if I'm not spiritual enough, then I'm probably not good enough either. Do I have to tell those of you in Christian leadership that you pretty much have to be perfect? If you play major league baseball, you can make millions batting .300 or more, which means, conversely, that you will be "out" about 70 percent of the times you step up to the plate to swing your bat. But in the ministry, the unwritten rule is that you should be batting something like .900 plus.

Our behavior is under constant scrutiny both in and out of the church. Maybe that's why people are so surprised to see me in shorts. Who else would notice? In the Catholic church—and in many mainline Protestant churches—pastors wear robes and other holy garments, not shorts.

To this day, more than forty years later, I still have mental and emotional etchings of the moments after church when I shook hands with our Lutheran pastor: my grandfather! Those robes just made me wilt. It was my grandpa in there, but not the grandpa who took me to baseball games in the summer. That was a more human grandpa.

Now hold on; I'm not crusading for casual dress in the house of God. Whether or not your tradition uses vestments is a moot point, and here's my point: Regardless of the "dress code" of our particular expression of faith, all of us in ministry wear vestments of one kind or another. If nothing else, your vestment is "the way I'm supposed to act because I'm a pastor."

I've seen it: Lutheran pastors seem to act one way, Assemblies of God leaders another, Southern Baptists still another. Can't you just hear the peculiar "accents" of our spiritual "languages"? Just listen once to how many ways preachers in different denominations can say the word *God.*

■ Family's Not Good Enough

If people aren't scrutinizing your life, your spouse or children are in the sniper's sight. My dear wife has said to me on countless occasions, "I'm not sure I'm what a minister's wife is supposed be." What's that? And who's supposed to determine what that is? Anybody and everybody? Exactly as many times as my wife has raised the issue, I've said to her, "Be yourself." And, really, that's what she is, and people love her for it.

Did you somehow understand me to say that ministers don't have to concern themselves with being examples to their flocks? If you did, I have not been making myself very clear. I believe deeply in what the Bible teaches:

> In everything set them an example by doing what is good. In your teaching show integrity, seriousness and soundness of speech that cannot be condemned, so that those who oppose you may be ashamed because they have nothing bad to say about us.
>
> Titus 2:7–8

Yes, to whom much is given, much is required, but I've found extraordinary peace knowing that being an example does not mean I have to be a *perfect* example. Do you know, by the way, why God uses imperfect people? He can't find any other kind.

Paul obviously came to this conclusion as well, because though he was an example of godliness to the people under his care, it's evident that he could never live up to everyone's expectations. From time to time we hear him defending himself by redefining the expectations people may have had for him. Content with what God called him to be, Paul seems to have had a healthy sense of who he was and wasn't:

> For when one says, "I follow Paul," and another, "I follow Apollos," are you not mere men? What, after all, is Apollos? And what is Paul? Only servants, through whom you came to believe—as the Lord has assigned to each his task. I planted the seed, Apollos watered it, but God made it grow. So neither

he who plants nor he who waters is anything, but only God, who makes things grow. The man who plants and the man who waters have one purpose, and each will be rewarded according to his own labor.

1 Cor. 3:4–8

■ Not Successful Enough

The megachurch is both a blessing and a curse. I should know. I have one, but mostly it has me. A pastor friend of a small church said to me once, "Other pastors just dream of what you're doing." And I told him, "Yeah, and I have nightmares." Another pastor of a small church asked very sincerely, "Does it give you a deep sense of fulfillment and personal accomplishment to know that you are preaching to several thousand people?"

I chuckled and said, "No, not really. Actually, it makes me really tired."

I confess I feel blessed to lead a large church, but (here I go being human) when I visit churches that are even larger, like Willow Creek or Saddleback or Phoenix First Assembly, I feel discouraged. Yes, *discouraged*, because I think I can and should do so much better, and if I'm feeling this, I know pastors of smaller churches are feeling it too. The megachurch/church growth movement has put extraordinary pressure on all of us, because it has essentially redefined the role of the pastor and how we measure ministry success. Megachurches have created a gap between what so many *are*—as God has made them and called them—and what church growth conferences are telling us we *should be*.

I teach church growth. I think we have a lot to learn from each other about how to be more effective in ministry, but "we do not dare to classify or compare ourselves with some who commend themselves. When they measure themselves by themselves and compare themselves with themselves, they are not wise" (2 Cor. 10:12). Some people have five talents, some two, some one. Our goal in life, then, is not to go for more talents, but to be faithful with the ones we have.

■ So Who's Defining You?

So what's your point of reference? Who are you trying to be like? Who's defining what you should look like, be like, act like? And as a result, what unrealistic expectations do you, consciously or unconsciously, put on your spouse and children?

And how are you feeling about your "role"? Overwhelmed? The statistics in chapter 3 are like machine-gun fire, ripping apart every little hope we may have about the future of our profession. And the larger question, which is the reason Al and I are writing this book: Who can you talk to about all this? Where do you find your support? Where can you be human without somebody putting pressure on you not to be "like that" because you're a pastor? Larry Crabb writes about "the safest place on earth." As a leader, do you have a place like that? If you don't, Al and I fear you will be unable to create a safe place for the people in your congregation. And that leads me to what is perhaps the most important principle of this book: We need more than preaching and teaching to become like Jesus. We need each other.

■ How Jesus Did Ministry

Earlier in this chapter I took you back to the first meeting between Jesus and a couple of his new followers. "Where do you live?" they asked him. "Come and see," he replied. This particular story is typical of Jesus' peripatetic ministry, a model for spiritual formation rarely practiced today. The term *peripatetic* is derived from a compound Greek word that means "to walk around." Simply, Jesus taught people as he lived with people—no "formal" training, no classrooms, no ecclesiastic buildings. Jesus' disciples learned ministry in the edifice of life and under the canopy of experience.

The early church picked up on this. After Pentecost thousands who had come to Christ devoted themselves to four things: the apostles' teaching, fellowship, the breaking of bread, and prayer (Acts 2:42). Note in particular the use of the term *devoted*. That particular word in Acts 2:42 has always gripped me, and it seems even stronger in the Greek, where the term means "devote oneself to," "continue in," "keep close company with," even "persevere." Furthermore, the term as it is used in this text is in the linear tense, which means that the devotion of these early Christians to teaching, shared-life, and prayer was uninterrupted, constant, and unceasing.

- They *kept devoting* themselves to the apostles' teaching, or truth.
- They *kept devoting* themselves to fellowship (Greek, *koinonia*), that is, sharing life together, having everything in common. They were committed to deep interpersonal, interdependent relationships.
- They *kept devoting* themselves to the breaking of bread, that is, they met from house to house and ate with one another. In the context of Middle Eastern life, to eat with someone was to accept that person fully into one's life and family. To eat together was more than just sharing a meal. It had overtones of a covenantal act. Moreover, the reference to "breaking bread" may suggest, as many New Testament scholars believe, that the early Christians shared the Lord's Table with one another at those meals.
- They *kept devoting* themselves to prayer. They invited the presence, blessing, guidance, and grace of God into every activity.

■ How People Change and Grow

Some of George Barna's recent findings about how people change have troubling implications. He found that several things contribute to change and growth in the lives of Christians, one of which is preaching. He wrote, "Sermons do not change most people."[1]

We keep preaching and teaching our brains out, though, presuming that people are listening to us and doing what we say! We may tell ourselves that other things are more important than sermonizing, yet our churches spend most of their time and money on weekend services and buildings to accommodate them. I should know. Our church has spent millions on facilities, and right now, as I'm writing this book, we are in the middle of building another one.

Certainly we can't throw the baby out with the baptistry. We need our buildings, and surely we need to teach and preach God's Word. Remember, the *first* thing to which the early Christians *devoted* themselves was "the apostles' teaching," and they borrowed buildings to do it. But we can't teach "the whole counsel of God" without doing the whole counsel of God, without devoting ourselves to the other elements of Christian formation: friendship, shared-life, and prayer.

■ The Transformation Triangle

Using a triangle, we have developed a simple model to highlight the four objects of devotion in the early church (see figure 4.1). At the top is preaching and teaching, the "apostles' doctrine," or truth. For the purposes of the diagram, we are using the term *truth* comprehensively to refer to everything God expects us to believe and do.

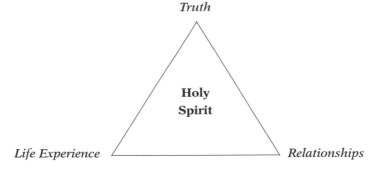

But hearing and knowing truth isn't an end in itself, as Jesus suggested at the conclusion of the Sermon on the Mount. He said that those "who hear these words of mine and put them into practice" are wise and find their security in him (Luke 7:24–25). Not only does research like Barna's show that hearing the truth affects us only somewhat, but it's often said that people don't even remember 90 percent of what they hear. What to do? Shut down Sunday services? It would save a lot of time and money! But we all know that's not realistic. It wouldn't even be right!

Although Barna found that sermons change people a little, he did discover that two things change people a lot: crisis and significant mentoring relationships. He wrote, "The greatest faith-related change happens in response to a cataclysmic event in a person's life . . . coupled with a strong and credible relationship with a believer who gives guidance during the period of trauma. Mentoring beats preaching in most cases."[2] Rick Warren says much the same thing in his best-selling book *The Purpose-Driven Life*: "God uses his Word, people, and circumstances to mold us. All three are indispensable for character development. God's Word provides the *truth* we need to grow, God's people provide the *support* we need to grow, and circumstances provide the *environment* we need to practice Christlikeness. . . . Many people assume all that's needed for spiritual growth is Bible study and prayer. But some issues in life will *never* be changed by Bible study or prayer alone. God uses people."[3]

The other two points of our triangle suggest this by two of the four objects of devotion in Acts 2:42: *koinonia* (shared-life) and breaking bread together, that is, welcoming people into the most personal and private rooms of your life.

Change is painful, and few people change when you simply tell them the truth—even if you yell at them! How heartily you will agree if you are a parent! People don't change—not you, not I, not our children—unless there are consequences for not changing. As I said earlier, people change when it becomes more painful to stay the same than to change, which is why the Bible teaches that our faith must be tested, *will* be tested.

Pain leads to change. In one of the not-so-popular passages of the Bible, James writes: *"Consider it pure joy,* my brothers, whenever you face trials of many kinds, because you know that the testing of your faith develops perseverance. Perseverance must finish its work so that you may be mature and complete, not lacking anything"* (James 1:2–4, italics mine).

It's unarguably clear from this and many other Bible texts that hardship is a necessary component of the Christian life. As Paul wrote, "I want *to know Christ* and the power of his resurrection and the fellowship of sharing in his sufferings, becoming like him in his death" (Phil. 3:10). Becoming like Christ is not possible outside the school of life. To bend a statement I've made a couple of times in this chapter, *we need more than preaching and teaching to become like Jesus. We need hardship.* "Endure *hardship* as discipline; God is treating you as sons. For what son is not disciplined by his father?" (Heb. 12:7).

■ The Science of Hardship

In his remarkable book *Primal Leadership,* Daniel Goleman of Harvard Business School articulates how we have literally been created to learn from experience. Goleman, best known for his book on emotional intelligence—how we handle ourselves and our relationships—explains how the brain's limbic system governs our feelings, impulses, and drives. Research shows that life skills based in the limbic areas "are best learned through motivation, extended practice, and feedback." Compare that kind of learning with what goes on in the neocortex, which governs analytical and technical ability.

> The neocortex grasps concepts quickly, placing them within an expanding network of associations and comprehension. This part of the brain, for instance, can figure out from reading a book how to use a computer program. . . . When learning technical skill or analytic skills, the neocortex operates with magnificent efficiency.

Goleman adds, "The problem is most training programs for enhancing emotional intelligence abilities, such as leadership, target the neocortex rather than the limbic brain. Thus, learning is limited and sometimes can even have a negative impact."[4]

The application of this understanding of the human brain has extraordinary implications for how we do ministry. People hear the truth in church, and some read their Bibles faithfully. The conceptual truth elements of the Christian life are learned fairly quickly, but when life hits the fan, people in our churches do not seem to have the ability to apply conceptual truth to their personal life issues. And more often than not they have no one to guide and support them through the anger, confusion, and pain. Not only are people often disconnected from significant relationships in their church (most of our people "just come on the weekend"), but they are likely to have more significant relationships *outside* the church, relationships that do not affirm the teaching of the Bible.

Finally, the fourth component of spiritual life to which the early Christians devoted themselves was prayer. Like the term *truth,* we are using the word *prayer* comprehensively. I define prayer as inviting the presence, power, guidance, and grace of God into every element of life, making sure that Jesus is Lord of every circumstance and every attitude in my heart about every circumstance. Thus the Holy Spirit is in the center of our transformation triangle.

■ Gnarly

Gnarly. That's what one of my best friends called me earlier this year. He was right, but like hearing your own voice on an audiocassette, you don't really know what your life is sounding like unless you have a brave and trusted friend to tell you. Your first reaction, of course, is to protest, "My voice doesn't *really* sound like that, does it? My life isn't *really* sounding that way, is it?"

"Yes, it is," my friend insisted. "Gnarly."

When I heard him say that, I had to pause a moment and tell myself, "He's right. I don't like hearing the word *gnarly* to describe my demeanor, but he's my good friend, he has my best interests in mind, I've invited him to speak into my life, so he must be right."

I was experiencing growing uncertainty and confusion about my role as senior minister of Word of Grace Church. I've been serving here for twenty years, during which time we have conducted four multimillion-dollar capital stewardship campaigns. I've been told that most pastors don't survive one. Writing new sermons and preaching every week, leading a staff of more than a hundred workers, meeting organizational challenges, and facing a bizarre legal problem only added to my spiritual and emotional restlessness.

Yep, I was gnarly—and wondering if maybe God was nudging me to move on. A number of factors caused me to think that it may be time for a change: Our married children and grandchildren were living in California—my wife's home state; I had an increasing number of invitations to speak in conferences; I was enticed by the thought of having more time to write; and, I confess, sometimes I was just sick and tired of sweltering in the oppressive Arizona summer heat. A lay leader in our church even asked one of my associate pastors, "Does Gary feel trapped?" My stress was bleeding into my leading.

So I asked for an evening with my friends: a few from my church board and staff; a neighbor; a pastor from Austin, Dan Davis; and a dear friend, Len Griffin, the pastor of a small church. Friends for decades who know me better than I know myself, they prayed and gave my wife and me priceless counsel.

In just one evening with significant friends, my bending life bent back straight. I laid to rest the notion of relocating, and I have a renewed focus and enthusiasm about the next ten years of leadership at our church. Not once did I have the sense that my friends were trying to talk me into or out of anything. Simply, they sensitively but objectively reaffirmed the calling of God in this season of my life: to stay rooted at Word of Grace while exploring other opportunities for ministry, especially the encouragement and support of other pastors and Christian leaders. In my season of doubt and questioning (crisis), I needed godly counsel (truth) from trustworthy friends (relationship). It worked!

■ The Acts 2:42 Ministry Model

What I have shared with you about my early fifties identity crisis, I trust, illustrates for you the Acts 2:42 ministry model. The "apostles' doctrine" part I know fairly well. I'm a mature pastor with two seminary degrees, but I know that I don't fully know myself, and when I'm in crisis (the last couple of years have been one of the three most challenging seasons of my life), I can't just single-handedly hack a trail through the tangle of my own thoughts and passions. *I need friends.* I need people who will break bread and share their lives with me. And all of us together need to devote ourselves to prayer, to ensure that we are as close as possible to knowing God's will.

Now more than ever Christians must devote themselves to shared-life, and Al and I are convinced it has to start with leaders who devote themselves to one another. Pastors may be deeply committed to the people in their church, but they are in most cases not dedicated to fully shared-life with their peers. We pastors are often isolated, lone rangers without the kinds of deep relational support systems necessary to sustain us in our extraordinarily difficult profession.

Even though God said, "It is not good for man [pastors?] to be alone," 70 percent or more of those in full-time ministry acknowledge they don't have one person they consider to be a very close friend. If that's the case, how do any of us in spiritual leadership obey the command in James 5:16 to "confess your sins to each other and pray for each other so that you may be healed"? And if we pastors aren't fully experiencing this element of New Testament community, if we leaders are friendless and, by default, not deeply accountable, it will be impossible for us to model authentic biblical community for the people whom God has called us to serve.

Modeling Failure

"And when you have turned back, strengthen your brothers."

—Luke 22:32

It was late Saturday afternoon, less than an hour before our evening service. I (Gary) had my car keys in hand to make the five-minute drive from my home to the church, but on the way out to the garage, I grabbed some important personal documents to drop into our little floor safe.

Five right. Twelve left. Three times back to fifty-one. Click. The safe popped open and, *Oh, no!* It was full of swampy water! And floating in the ooze were my best baseball cards.

Our water heater had burst about three months before, and thinking the water had made its way out of the house one way, I discovered to my dismay that it had seeped through a wall and filled my floor safe.

Arrrgh! What am I going to do? I thought. And then reality hit: "I have to *preach* in an hour!" I moaned aloud. For the moment I wasn't exactly thinking about God—or all his dear people on their way to church that evening to hear me talk about God's

75

love for them. All I could think about was my precious baseball cards and priceless family memorabilia marinating in that primordial soup. I took everything out to dry (as if that would do any good!) and headed off to do my pastor job.

And my text that night? You won't believe it. James, specifically chapter 1: "Consider it pure joy, my brothers, whenever you face trials of many kinds, because you know that the testing of your faith develops perseverance" (vv. 2–3). Yeah, that one. Man, did I have a gripping introduction to my sermon. I can't remember a time when the congregation listened so intently—well, except maybe the day I came to church after having the fight of my life with my brother.

■ So Much to Teach and Nothing to Say

There's no point in my telling that story, except to say that we've not had such a falling out before or since. And it involved my mother, my children, and my wife. You know how family problems are—like, well, a floor safe full of stagnant, smelly water. And that weekend my sermon topic was how to manage your anger. Imagine me preaching about managing anger when I was as angry as I have ever been.

I suppose the wise thing to do would have been to pull out some old sermon notes (I have drawers full of those) and tell everyone that God had led me to preach about something else. But I didn't. I couldn't. I simply began my message by telling everyone the truth. I confessed my anger and my helplessness to manage it. I told the congregation that the last thing I wanted to do was to be in church that weekend and preach, let alone talk about anger management.

Yet it turned out to be one of the most powerful and effective preaching experiences of my life—and so healing for me as we closed each service with the Lord's Supper and encountered God's presence in the cup and the bread. I wept at the end of each of our three weekend services. John Maxwell would call this "failing forward."

■ "But You Should Hear My Story"

Some of you could tell far more traumatic and significant stories, I'm sure, like my friend John Vawter, former seminary president and one of my doctor of ministry professors. Deciding he wanted to return to local church ministry (he had done that for years before his work in the academic community), he accepted the senior pastor position at a prominent Bible church in our area. On his first Sunday in his new pulpit, he and his wife found out his adult daughter was doing heroin.

Do you *really* believe that all things work together for good for those who love God? Here's John's story: He remained the pastor of that church for several years, his daughter experienced an extraordinary personal miracle and has been clean for years, and John is speaking in pastors' conferences all over the country about healing for people in ministry whose children are doing drugs.[1] This is another example of failing forward.

The cover of the September 24, 2001, issue of *Time* features President Bush holding high a small American flag over the rubble of the World Trade Center. Inside is a brief editorial, "A President Finds His Voice," by Margaret Carlson. She writes:

> A man ain't supposed to cry . . . but the President didn't begin to fill the role of Commander in Chief until he let his eyes well up. . . . [He] said, "I am a loving guy. . . . This country will not relent until we have saved ourselves and others from the terrible tragedy that came upon America." This transcendent moment erased two days in which Bush blinked his way through TelePrompTered remarks like a school boy reciting his lesson . . . but this . . . was . . . followed by the very first good Bush moment, in which he showed his humanity.[2]

So pastor, if you're reading this, tell me, do you blink through your sermons like a schoolboy reciting a lesson? Or do you show your humanity? I have come to believe that *I am strongest when I am weak and weakest when I am strong*, another way to say:

To keep me from becoming conceited because of these surpass-
ingly great revelations, there was given me a thorn in my flesh, a
messenger of Satan, to torment me. Three times I pleaded with
the Lord to take it away from me. But he said to me, "My grace
is sufficient for you, for my power is made perfect in weakness."
Therefore I will boast all the more gladly about my weaknesses,
so that Christ's power may rest on me.

2 Corinthians 12:7–10

■ Shamed by a Chicken

Never forget that ministry is not about what you've done
or who you are. It's about who you aren't—and God's grace
working through your weakness. Like all of us in ministry, the
apostle Peter learned this the hard way. Jesus had said,

"Simon, Simon, Satan has asked to sift you as wheat. But I have
prayed for you, Simon, that your faith may not fail. And when
you have turned back, strengthen your brothers."
But he replied, "Lord, I am ready to go with you to prison
and to death."
Jesus answered, "I tell you, Peter, before the rooster crows
today, you will deny three times that you know me."

Luke 22:31–34

This passage from the New Testament, one I cherish deeply,
has five simple lessons for all of us in Christian ministry:

1. *The ministry will be difficult because Satan will sift your
soul:* "Simon, Simon, Satan has asked to sift you as wheat. . . ."
Adam and Eve were tempted. Jesus was tempted. You will be
tempted, sometimes in extraordinary ways. I told a graduat-
ing class at a seminary commencement recently that this is
"seminary from hell." I will share my own bout with the devil
in the next chapter.

2. *Whatever success you have in ministry is rooted in the fact
that Jesus is praying for you:* "Simon, Simon, Satan has asked
to sift you as wheat. But I have prayed for you, Simon, that

your faith may not fail." Replace Simon's name with your own and imagine Jesus speaking to you. Remember that anytime God has to call your name twice, you're in trouble. You can be confident, though, that Jesus is praying for your future right now.

What a comfort that Jesus not only knows what you've done in your past and has forgiven you for it, but he also knows precisely what you are going to do in the future, and he's praying for that. He offers you his unconditional mercy for your past and his unconditional grace for your future.

3. *Human effort and the pride of personal success die hard:* "Simon, Simon, Satan has asked to sift you as wheat. . . ." But Peter replied, "Lord, I am ready to go with you to prison and to death." Bad idea, Pete. Ain't gonna happen that way, because (and this is my fourth point):

4. *You will make mistakes, sometimes grievous ones, when it is pretty obvious to you and your friends that your mistakes were sin:* "No," Jesus insisted, "I tell you, Peter, before the rooster crows today, you will deny three times that you know me." No, this is not negative. This passage is about the most important lesson any of us can ever learn: Ministry is not about me, it's about Christ in me. "I have been crucified with Christ," Paul said, "and I no longer live, but Christ lives in me. The life I live in the body, I live by faith in the Son of God, who loved me and gave himself for me" (Gal. 2:20). My life as a minister must be, more than anything else, a daily message about amazing grace.

5. *Ministry is not about who you are or what you've done, but about what you aren't:* "I have prayed for you, Simon, that your faith may not fail. And when you have turned back, strengthen your brothers." To me, this is one of the most incredible statements in the Bible. Tell me, how can you strengthen the brothers when you've just had the worst night of your life? You've made a fool of yourself! You've denied Christ. How can you go out and strengthen somebody else after you've done that?

I'll tell you how: Tell them that the reason you're here today to tell your story, the reason your faith didn't fail—even though you may have given everyone around you a reason to think it did—is because *Jesus prayed for you.* You see, if in the dark night of your life you did all the right things, just like Jesus, then your testimony, essentially, would be about *you,* how *you* did it, how *you* rose to the occasion, how *you* stood your ground.

Certainly, there are times when all of us need to be an example to others. But when I do *nothing,* or, like Peter, I do the very things I promise never to do, and somehow I survive the night, it's not about me. I can't boast except for the grace of God working for me in spite of me. Personally, I have had plenty of those times in my life to convince me that *everything* is in God's hands. At any given moment in time, it may seem like God is neutral, distant, just waiting in his holy heaven to see what I'm going to do, as if everything that happens in my life is up to me. But Proverbs 16:9 suggests otherwise: "In his heart a man plans his course, but the LORD determines his steps" (Prov. 16:9).

God really is in control of my circumstances, but more, he's just as much in control of me. Jesus is loving me, praying for me, and sustaining me, even when I'm making a fool of myself. Grace isn't grace if it starts with me.

■ A Successful Fragile Man

I'm a fragile man, and I have only momentary illusions about my role in my success. The truth of the matter is that *Jesus keeps praying for me,* and this is certainly the key to my success. Yes, I could give you reasons why my life has been successful. I have three graduate degrees, I'm the senior pastor of a megachurch, and this is my eighth book. I can give you a stack of suggestions on how to grow your church, and some of them might even work for you. But when I look back on my life, I see the strong hand of God. You see, I've had far more reasons for not being successful:

- I was a nobody in high school and college. For example, I earned a C in simpleton English my freshman year in high school, and in my sophomore year, my English teacher read my first paper to the entire class as an example of really bad writing.

- I have had to overcome an extraordinary fear of public speaking. It's a demon that still snarls at me from time to time.

- I am, at times, emotionally fragile, and my friends and family would tell you that I can be terribly self-absorbed.

- I've had depression off and on and have taken medication for it. Our family has had a medical history of depression, and one of my uncles, at the age of thirty-seven, had to retire from the ministry because he could not overcome the darkness in his soul.

- And as I mentioned in the first chapter (and will share more in subsequent chapters), about fifteen years ago I was diagnosed with an incurable, terminal heart condition. At this point my cardiologist tells me I'm fine. Maybe my initial diagnosis was incorrect. Maybe God healed me.

Like Peter, I really have nothing to say about myself and everything to say about Jesus. Like Mary, I see how God "has been mindful of the humble state of his servant" (Luke 1:48). I feel like Paul, who referred to himself as "one abnormally born." He added: "For I am the least of the apostles and do not even deserve to be called an apostle, because I persecuted the church of God. But by the grace of God I am what I am, and his grace to me was not without effect. . . . We have this treasure in jars of clay to show that this all-surpassing power is from God and not from us" (1 Cor. 15:8–10; 2 Cor. 4:7).

If, like Peter, you fail, Jesus knows in advance that it is going to happen. Before the fall, he'll pray for you. After the fall, he'll be there to pick you up. When he does, as Jesus instructed Peter, *strengthen the brothers.* The life of the Christian leader is never private. It's not so much that we have a public life, that a lot of people know us and scrutinize our behaviors. Rather, we are inseparably linked to the people we have been called to serve, and God has called us to "strengthen the brothers" out of the grace working in our own lives.

■ Modeling Failure

It's unavoidable: We are role models, "examples to the flock" (1 Peter 5:3), certainly of righteousness, obedience, and faith, but also examples of how to find grace, forgiveness, and even *strength* when we fail. We must model how to fail forward, how to turn our failures into success, because most of the people in our congregations are not successful, and those who are doing well often wrestle with the demons of discontent. Most are struggling with life and experiencing emotional pain. Have you ever prayed with a small group of people? *Everyone* will have a special request, usually one that's fairly urgent. Life is difficult even under the best of circumstances.

Family, work, health, finances, home or business ownership, and even just driving to work can be stressful. People walk into the house of God with extraordinary burdens. On any given Sunday a good number of the families in your congregation probably have had an argument on the way to church. So the last thing they need from us spiritual leaders is an irrelevant or high-handed spirituality. They need someone who cares, "a high priest who is [able] to sympathize with our weaknesses . . . so that we may receive mercy and find grace to help us in our time of need" (Heb. 4:15–16).

Herein lies the positive power of failure, the benefit of failing forward. It's in my glaring weakness, greatest loss, and worst failure that I'm brought to my knees to find God's extravagant grace. And that's what people in my church need so desperately—grace to help in time of need. I find God at the point of my greatest helplessness, which brings us back to Paul's peculiar definition of success: "I will not boast about myself, except about my weaknesses. . . . But he said to me, 'My grace is sufficient for you, for my power is made perfect in weakness.' Therefore I will boast all the more gladly about my weaknesses, so that Christ's power may rest on me. That is why, for Christ's sake, I delight in weaknesses" (2 Cor. 12:5, 9–10).

I *delight* in my *weaknesses*? What kind of an example to the flock is that? How utterly nonpastoral! How could Paul think this way? He explains: "I delight in weaknesses, in insults, in hardships, in persecutions, in difficulties. *For when I am weak, then I am strong*" (2 Cor. 12:9–10, italics mine). There's a wonderful logic in this. It works this way:

> A lot of me, and a little God.
> A little of me, and a little less than all of God.
> None of me, and all of God.

■ Depressed in Hawaii

I've been to Hawaii nearly every year since the late 1980s. Not for vacation. No, never for something human like that. I've gone for only one reason: to teach the Bible for Youth With A Mission (YWAM). Okay, I confess. I'm writing a book about being authentic, so I should admit that I have mixed motives teaching the Bible in Hawaii.

Students at YWAM's University of the Nations come literally from all over the world, and I always have to needle them about how they knew it was God's will for them to attend a discipleship school *in Hawaii*. I've told classes there, tongue in cheek, that the only students in the class who are certainly in the perfect will of God are the ones who actually live in Hawaii. Everyone else, I tell them, came mostly for God and a lot for Hawaii.

Hawaii is a beautiful place, and people there shouldn't be depressed, but as I mentioned earlier, I've struggled with depression off and on—even in Hawaii. So being my typically candid self, I mentioned to the class that even though everything in my life was going great, I was feeling down, and I spoke briefly about how I serve God obediently in spite of my pain.

At the end of the week, when the leaders of the discipleship school asked the students to give me feedback on my five days with them, a middle-aged woman stood up and, looking at me with teary eyes, said, "The most meaningful moment in the week of teaching for me was when you confessed that you, a successful person, struggle with depression."

Amazing. My depression confession was an incidental comment in twelve hours of teaching. I had shared so many deep insights, I thought, so many liberating principles. But what touched one woman's heart more than anything was my openness. She heard a man of God, a role model, a successful pastor, acknowledge his weakness, and she found grace to help her in her time of need.

It goes without saying that when we talk about "failing forward," we are not suggesting that Christian leaders should live a life of sin just to be good examples of God's love and forgiveness! No, there's a fine line here. Leaders must be candid about themselves, about their own need for God's grace. *Authenticity* is the word *du jour.* But to the extent that a leader is self-revealing, he or she risks undermining the confidence people feel in his or her leadership. Personally, in public ministry I am as transparent about my life as I can be. I would rather err on the side of authenticity, and privately I must be utterly open with a small number of trusted friends in the spirit of James 5:16: "Confess your sins to each other and pray for each other so that you may be healed. The prayer of a righteous man is powerful and effective" (James 5:16).

In *Primal Leadership,* Daniel Goleman tells us that transparency "is not only a leadership virtue, but an organizational strength. Transparency—an authentic openness to others about one's feelings, beliefs, and actions—allows integrity, or the sense that a leader can be trusted."[3] Honesty really is the best policy!

■ Wounded Healers

You likely have heard the expression "wounded healers." That's what we spiritual leaders are—people who have been forgiven and healed showing others how they can be forgiven and healed. In an article from *The Journal of Psychosocial Nursing* titled "Meeting the Spiritual Needs in an Inpatient Unit," Mary D. Moller offers practical suggestions from "hospitalized consumers," many of whom had "expressed intense distress and chagrin at the concept of religion as at least half . . . had been 'evicted' from their home church due to symptoms caused by their psychiatric disabilities." Here are just a few of her suggestions. Notice how they are grace-based.

- Let me know you care. You can convey this by saying something like "I'm sorry this has happened to you." That will make me feel like you respect me.
- Accept me. I do not expect you to meet all my needs, just accept me and talk to me.
- Be real, not authoritative. Please don't give me trivia or contrived answers, because it makes me feel betrayed and it will feel like you are giving me lip service.
- No sermons. Do not give me theological reasons why I'm the way I am—I can't understand sermons when I'm psychotic.[4]

It would be a stretch to say that just about everyone in church is psychotic; in fact, it would be wrong in the clinical meaning of the term. But whether or not people are psychotic, they don't always understand sermons. Yes, good teaching is essential. We must *devote* ourselves to the "apostles' teaching," but mostly people want grace to come through us in their time of need.

■ But How?

Healing people out of your own personal healing isn't something you can just make up. If you did, it would be the worst sort of hypocrisy. Imagine pretending to be real! No, grace has to happen to you. Being real with others begins with getting real with yourself. Tell me, where is this happening with pastors, among pastors? Where do Christian leaders confess their sins? Where can they be real? Open and safe? And healed? The answer: Leaders need leaders, pastors need pastors, not only for professional guidance and support, but for life. Paul D.

Stanley and leadership guru J. Robert Clinton of Fuller Seminary write:

> A network . . . of relationships is *not an option* for a believer who desires to grow, minister effectively and continuously, and finish well. *It is imperative!* In our studies of leaders, we can clearly conclude with few exceptions that those who experienced anointed ministry and finished well had a significant network of meaningful relationships that inspired, challenged, listened, pursued, developed, and held one another accountable. Those that failed to reach full maturity and finish well did not have it, or cut all or part of it off at some point. *We have personally determined that we will develop and maintain an active relational network for ourselves and pay whatever cost is necessary to do it.*[5]

In the next chapter, I (Gary) share my personal journey out of the illusion and isolation of pastoral role playing, through pain and loss, and into the reality of self-awareness and the safety of deep friendships. Jesus saved my soul, but Al (and other friends) saved my life.

Al Saved My Life

The pleasantness of one's friend springs from his earnest counsel.

—Proverbs 27:9

"Leaders have to *invite* accountability."

—Bill Hybels

I was drowning in the deep blue sea.

Not literally, of course, but my life was at a crossroads, and my future looked bleak.

Literally, though, I (Gary) was standing on a beach in Hawaii. Recall from chapter 5 that I wrote about how I *have* to go there about once a year to do the will of God. And I told about how I was sort of depressed—right there in Hawaii. Well, now I'm flashing back to my very first visit to the islands. I was really depressed then. Suffocating in personal despair, I was in the front end of the worst year of my life. My troubles had only just begun, but I was already feeling like leaving the ministry. Because of a number of things that had happened in the previous couple of months, I was thinking that God himself was finished with me. "Maybe he's releasing me to do something else with my life," I thought.

There I was, standing on huge Hapuna Beach on the big island of Hawaii. A typically gorgeous stretch of Hawaiian coast, the place was untypically deserted. Only a handful of people were sunning themselves on a half mile of glistening white sand. "Why so few?" I wondered.

Maybe the warning posted on a huge sign between the parking area and the beach had something to do with it:

DANGEROUS CURRENTS

If you get caught in the current, don't swim against it.

Let it carry you out to sea.

It will dissipate, and you will be able to swim back to shore.

Right there in front of that sign, I had an overwhelming sense of God's presence. I "heard" his voice in the caution: "DANGEROUS CURRENTS." I was in one and flailing against it, resisting people who were resisting me and sinking in the sea of my own helplessness and pain. God was telling me to let go and allow the currents of life to carry me away from the safety of the shoreline into the unknown but certain future he had prepared for my life.

■ The Dark Night of My Soul

I referred to this "defining moment" of my life in the opening chapter of this book. Like a divorce, years of important relationships ended, people on my staff died, and at the age of thirty-eight I was diagnosed with what was thought to be a life-threatening heart condition—all in about ten months. I could write *two* books about the bizarre things that happened and what people did and said, but that would serve no purpose.

You see, my hardships and suffering—the injustices in my life—are "common to man" (1 Cor. 10:13), and many of you have faced worse. If you want to read about an especially troubled life, try Paul's in 2 Corinthians 11:23–28. But like the apostle of grace, I can tell you in just a handful of words why everything happened to me that year: "If I must boast, I will boast of the things that show my weakness" (2 Cor. 11:30). At the very bitter end of myself, I learned firsthand—I *experienced*—two of the most essential components of the "perfect" Christian life: (1) self-awareness and (2) the necessity of mentoring friendships.

■ Self-Awareness

For the first time in my life, as a result of the worst time in my life, I came to know myself—and to understand how my behaviors were affecting other people, both for good and for evil. Previously, I had been able to see only the good side.

Seeing the dark side of my soul is difficult, because denial is one of the terrible consequences of human sin. Undoubtedly you know the story: Adam and Eve disobeyed God, which set in motion a now-common human behavioral pattern of avoiding the truth at all costs: "The woman you put here with me—she gave me some fruit from the tree, and I ate it" (Gen. 3:12). In one brief, clever sentence, Adam mocked God, slammed his wife, and essentially absolved himself of any responsibility for eating the forbidden fruit.

If I understand the not so subtle messages here, Adam is suggesting that God started the problem by creating the woman, the woman caused the problem by handing Adam the fruit, and Adam, considering the circumstances, was left without a choice: "I just ate it." Poor Adam couldn't help himself. He was a victim.

Pretty Good People

We have an infamous state penitentiary about fifty miles from our city, and people who have worked there have told me that virtually none of the convicts imprisoned there, some for life, believes that he is, plain and simple, guilty. And if people like that are not in touch with themselves, what about "pretty good people" like you and me?

Last week I think I ran a red light. I'm not sure (can you hear my denial?), but it was one of those cross streets with a camera, and I saw a very bright flash as I crossed into the intersection. I'm still not sure, because I haven't received a notice in the mail, but I fear it's on its way. Oh, does that annoy me! These are some of my thoughts:

> I wasn't speeding.
> My front tires were over the white line when I saw the flash.
> This has never happened to me before.
> I'm a good driver.
> I'm not like other rude people who speed up when they see the light change to yellow then race through the intersection at ludicrous speed.

When the notice comes, if it does come, do you think any of my deep thoughts will get me out of paying the fine? Cameras don't lie; people do. Maybe it would be more accurate to say that people don't lie; they have a fig leaf for just about everything.

Demons of Denial

A first cousin of sin, denial is endemic, and by its very nature, denial can't see itself. People who don't think they're in denial, or worse, people who never even think about if they might be, are in deep denial. Furthermore, I am convinced that the more resolute a person's denial systems, the more vulnerable that person is to spiritual attack and oppression.

I have pondered the spiritual implications of denial myself. I have even written a book about it, *Overcoming the Dominion of Darkness,* which I wrote shortly after my most difficult year.[1] To me it's highly significant that the first component of the armor of God in Ephesians 6 is the belt of truth. Many scholars are persuaded that this is not a reference to knowing doctrinal truth or knowing the Bible well. It is, rather, a reference to *truthfulness,* and the belt is to cover the most vulnerable parts of your life. As the psalmist prayed, "Surely you desire truth in the inner parts; you teach me wisdom in the inmost place" (Ps. 51:6).

Holy Cow

The story of Moses and Aaron is a case study in denial. As the prince of Egypt descended from the thunderheads swirling around the jagged desert mount, he saw that something was terribly wrong in the camp of the Israelites. They were worshiping a gilded cow! Moses was mystified, but his brother Aaron explained. Listen to Aaron's nonsense as Moses put him on the spot:

> "What did these people do to you, that you led them into such great sin?"
>
> "Do not be angry, my lord," Aaron answered. "You know how prone these people are to evil. They said to me, 'Make us gods who will go before us. As for this fellow Moses who brought us up out of Egypt, we don't know what has happened to him.' So I told them, 'Whoever has any gold jewelry, take it off.' Then they gave me the gold, and I threw it into the fire, and out came this calf!"
>
> Exodus 32:22–24

Yeah, right! The calf just "came out"? Aaron's story makes you shake your head in disbelief—just like people close to you might be doing as they talk about you behind your back.

My dark night of pain involved people shaking their heads in frustration and talking behind my back. My knee-jerk reaction at the time was to nip that disloyalty in the bud. But now I understand that, as the leader, I had unconsciously created my own troubled world, and I had no one to blame but myself. My elaborate systems of denial would not allow others to speak openly with me. Like a person in a twelve-step program, I realized . . .

I had a problem.

I was powerless over myself.

My life was out of control.

I needed a "Higher Power."

And I needed a sponsor, that is, a friend or several friends who would support me, let me share the deepest emotions of my heart, and speak the truth to me in love.

Obfuscation

Let me suggest another word for denial. Al introduced it to me: *obfuscation.* To obfuscate means "to make dark, obscure; to confuse." Of course I would never do that. I'm a pastor. I'm a bright human being. Thoughtful too. If anybody knows me, I know me. *Wrong!* The truth is that I'm pretty much the last person to know me.

Remember the first time you heard your voice on video- or audiocassette? You wanted to scream out in the voice you'd never really heard, "That's not my voice!" Oh, yes it is. All of your friends can hear what you've never heard: your own voice. The same thing can be said about your personality. Have you ever asked a friend, "Is that *really* the way I am?" hoping your friend would say no? But nodding his or her head sheepishly, your friend muttered something like, "Everybody who knows you says you're that way."

That's essentially what Al and other significant people[2] in my life were telling me during my difficult year. All of them were very encouraging about what I was doing right, and most of them also helped me see my dysfunctions, especially Al. He was relentless in asking me one of the most important questions in life: "What is God saying to *you?* What needs to change in *your* life?" Don't focus on what others are saying and doing, he kept telling me. Don't let the misunderstandings become the lord of your emotions. Don't think of yourself as a victim. In whatever way others may be at fault in this situation, you can't change them.

What is God saying to *you?*

Assessing Your Self-Understanding

So I read books like *Telling Yourself the Truth* by William Backus and Marie Chapian and *Self-Talk* by David Stoop. I journaled. I took a graduate class in counseling here in Phoenix from Dr. Bill Retts, who was very helpful in guiding me into a deeper understanding of who I am and who I am not. I prayed. I fasted three days at a time, and others prayed and fasted with me. I'd like to say that one morning the light went on in my soul, ending forever my dark night of pain, but nothing happened suddenly. At moments I felt hopelessly trapped, but God was working, and slowly but surely I came to a fairly healthy self-understanding.

How do I know? Because I've learned to ask all the significant people in my life for status reports on my attitudes and behaviors. Just yesterday I sat in my office reviewing my "360," a leadership assessment tool that compares what others (those over you, your peers, and those under you) think about you—and how that compares with how you think about yourself.[3] I was pleasantly surprised to see that my self-assessment was remarkably consistent with the assessment of those who work closely with me. At no point did I see myself in a better light than my peers, and in a couple instances, my colleagues scored me a little higher than I scored myself!

■ Mentoring Friendships

The problem with a blind spot is that you can't see it, but others can. That is why mentoring relationships aren't just a good idea; they are as leadership expert Robert Clinton says, "not an option" and "imperative," especially for leaders. Why? Because leaders struggle with denial more than anyone in the general population, and the reason is clear: The nature of leadership is to guide and direct other people. By the nature of their role, leaders are seldom in a place where they are being guided and directed.

People generally think leaders are usually or mostly right, and that's the way leaders perceive themselves, which makes it increasingly difficult for successful leaders to believe they are wrong. For this reason, leaders, even nice ones, can be some of the most difficult people to be around. Bill Hybels writes in his book *Courageous Leadership,* "We would rather try to inspire or control the behavior of others than face the rigorous work of self-reflection and inner growth."[4]

Using the Fear Stick

Many of you have heard someone say, "Touch not God's anointed," which comes from the Old Testament account of David and Saul. Saul was a bad king. David, on the other hand, was a pure-hearted, up-and-coming leader and king-to-be. Feeling insecure and threatened, Saul made several attempts to kill David. At two points David had Saul's life in his hands and could have killed him easily, but no, he couldn't do that, wouldn't do that, because Saul was "God's anointed" (see 1 Sam. 24:6; 26:9–11).

These stories have helped many young leaders wrestle down their ambitions and put their future in God's hands. But "touch not God's anointed" was David's declaration, not Saul's. When the leader has to fall back into the fortress of his or her position or title and warn whimpering followers, "Touch not God's anointed," he or she ceases to be the leader. As John Maxwell has said so many times, "Leadership is influence." Perhaps another way to say this is that "leadership is power," and power in the wrong hands is a terrible thing.

Philip Gourevitch wrote recently in the *New Yorker,* "Pol Pot [the infamous Cambodian 'killing fields' dictator] once said that when it comes to judging matters of right and wrong the answer is strength. Strength! If you possess strength, then you are right, and if you lack strength, then you are wrong."[5]

Jesus and the Gentiles

In striking contrast, Jesus taught us:

"The kings of the Gentiles lord it over them; and those who exercise authority over them call themselves Benefactors. [We're in trouble when leaders think they are doing us a favor.] But you are not to be like that. Instead, the greatest among you [the one with the most influence] should be like the youngest, and the one who rules like the one who serves. For who is greater, the one who is at the table or the one who serves? Is it not the one who is at the table? But I am among you as one who serves."

Luke 22:25–27

In other words, our influence as leaders is not derived from our position, but from our acts of service, from our willingness, like Jesus, to lay down our lives for the ones who follow us. Leadership is godly influence, not forceful posturing, intimidation, or manipulation. Hiding behind my position of authority is just another layer in my denial system. It allows me to stay in control (or so I think) and prevents me from hearing truth about myself and how I am perceived by others. Ironically, I am the most powerful when I am the most vulnerable: "That is why, for Christ's sake, I delight in weaknesses, in insults, in hardships, in persecutions, in difficulties. *For when I am weak, then I am strong*" (2 Cor. 12:10, italics mine).

Killing People with Our Kindness

Spiritual leadership compounds the denial problem, because we have God on our side. Most pastors don't pull out the "touch-not-God's-anointed" gun, but what's so difficult for us to see is how our role as a spiritual leader simply doesn't allow people in our sphere of influence to be honest with us. Leadership really is influence as we impact people around us unconsciously and indirectly.

Many people we lead and serve love us dearly, respect us deeply, and wouldn't dare criticize their pastor. For better or for worse, it's those most loyal to us who become our most trusted partners in ministry, but therein lies the problem. Their respect and loyalty make it very difficult for them to be honest with us, even when we invite them to be honest.

A recent international news event—sexual misconduct in the Roman Catholic Church—illustrates the danger of leadership in isolation, religious leaders hiding behind the robes of their profession. Pause to think about that. Pause to repent, because this isolation is not a problem exclusive to the Catholic church; it's a deep dysfunction in the soul of spiritual leadership. Not only do pastors shield themselves with their ministerial fig leaves, but they avoid significant mentoring relationships. We know this, because research shows that nearly four out of every five pastors do not have a network of close, mentoring friendships.

Without flinching, Al refers to this problem inherent in spiritual leadership as idolatry, putting the leader on a pedestal—and the leader allowing it to happen. Having been a pastor for many years, I've seen this again and again in the way people relate to me. We Christian leaders are quasi-celebrities, and we all know how people behave themselves around real celebrities. In fact, the rich and famous are affectionately called "idols"!

If as a spiritual leader you are not daily reminding yourself of this reality and making every effort to get real with the people you are leading, then you are probably in denial, perhaps even in danger of your leadership unraveling. The story can be told again and again: Everything in the church seems just fine. Everyone seems to be supporting the pastor, and then one day, *suddenly* it seems, all hell breaks loose. "Where did *that* come from? How did *that* happen?" church members ask. "How could such a fine man of God just crash?" But the "sudden" resignation of a wonderful pastor is never, in fact, sudden. It is nearly always the consequence of years of deeply rooted unhealthy and unrecognized patterns of behavior.

Drinking Our Bathwater

The sociology of leadership is such that we leaders tend to hire "team players," people who we presume think like we think and, more often than we know, tell us what we want to hear. As I heard prominent Houston pastor Kirbyjon Caldwell say at a Willow Creek Leadership Summit recently, "Leaders tend to surround themselves with people who will drink their bathwater." He added, "And the bigger the organization, the more leaders must get to the truth, the whole truth, and nothing but the truth." This is why I need my wife, my family, and good friends who do not relate to me in the context of my ministry or success. My mother has never told me what I want to hear!

Daniel Goleman, in his best-selling *Primal Leadership*, calls this a *CEO disease:* the information vacuum around a leader created when people withhold important (and usually unpleasant) information. This disease, he says, can be epidemic, and top leaders typically get the least reliable information about how they are doing. He writes:

> For instance, an analysis of 177 separate studies that assessed more than 28,000 managers found that feedback on performance became less consistent the higher the manager's position or the more complex the manager's role. . . . The higher leaders were in an organization, the greater the inflation rate—that is, the number of times they saw themselves as doing better on a competence than did those around them.[6]

Goleman also noted that self-awareness of leadership abilities was greatest for CEOs of the best-performing companies and poorest for CEOs of the worst performers. In other words, self-awareness and success are interrelated.

Smothered by His Personality

Not too long ago I spoke with a church leader in California who, some years earlier in his career, had worked on the staff of a megachurch. His face showed distress as he talked about how controlling his former pastor had been. Frankly, I was surprised to hear that, because I knew the guy he was talking about (I'm not sure he knew that I knew), and he did not strike me as controlling.

So I asked his former associate, "Why would you say that? Was he aggressive in some way at staff meetings? Demanding? Abusive from time to time?"

"No," he replied. "He just overwhelmed us with his magnetic personality, humor, and his ability to communicate."

A Salesman for God

Ouch! I felt pain as God spoke to me in that moment. I won't lay claim to the magnetic personality part, but I know how I can out-communicate and talk over other people, which is why for years I have had other people facilitate board and staff meetings. I'm a natural communicator, a salesman for God, not a facilitator of meetings. What works, though, in the pulpit—passionate, uninterrupted *monologue*—does not work in the board room or staff meeting, where *dialogue* is essential. Interactive, listening leaders

- rely on everyone on the team
- build consensus by drawing out the multiple gifts and perspectives on the team
- create a sense of ownership on the part of everyone on the team by welcoming everyone's full participation in the process of making important decisions

Where did I learn this stuff? *From Al!* A consummate facilitator (he has done it for large corporations and small churches), Al has coached me on how to lead meetings. I have avoided leading meetings at times for the sake of the wonderful people attending them. I want to spare them the pain of sitting through my monologues, but I can and do facilitate meetings. I've *learned* leadership. When I put my mind to it, I'm able to generate a lot of discussion, but this skill doesn't come naturally for me.

I'm what Daniel Goleman, author of *Emotional Intelligence,* refers to as a "pace-setting leader." I'm good at what I do. I push myself to accomplish tasks, and I'm self-critical. Unfortunately, I can unfairly apply my high standards to people around me. This has not been good for team building and collaboration.

Listening Power

Want to go out on a limb? Want to become a better leader? Want to be perceived as someone who listens? You may be surprised to know that people in your sphere of influence don't necessarily want to have it their way. Mostly, all of us just want to be heard, so one of the ways to influence people deeply is simply to ask them honestly for their opinion. Here are some starter questions:

- What do you think?
- What should I do?
- How can I make your job easier?
- How can I make you feel more supported in what you do?
- What are you hearing from other people in the church that I should hear?
- How can I be a better leader?
- How can I be a better person as a leader?

My former executive pastor, Bob Blayter, shared with me an incident in his life that illustrates the power of listening. Earlier in his ministry at another church, two families approached him the same week with opposing concerns. One said, "Bob, you need to relax when you preach. You are way too emotional." A few days later another family approached him: "Bob, you are way too relaxed when you preach. You need more passion." Suppressing his urge to laugh, Bob just smiled and thanked them. "I'll pray about that," he said sincerely.

I probably would have argued with both of them! But Bob essentially did nothing. How could he? It was a no-win situation. Bob won by listening. A couple weeks later he took the initiative to follow up. "How's my preaching lately? How am I doing?" he asked each couple. Both said, "You're doing just great, Bob!"

People just want to be heard. I'm not suggesting that we listen simply to appease people, with no intention to change, but this story illustrates the power of listening and that people in our care, both staff and church members, often want to be heard more than they want to force change. Always keep in mind, though, that often people on your leadership team have things to say that could change you and your organization forever.

My Future Depends on God and Andy

My associate Andy is a case in point. These post–9/11 years have been difficult for many organizations, and our church has been no exception. Our motto has become "more with less." As a result of increasing ministry demands coupled with decreasing income, our leadership team, in partnership with our governing board, committed itself to reinventing the way we do ministry. After weeks of organizational review meetings, though, we felt stuck, unable to think outside the organizational boxes. Sharing our dilemma with Andy Jackson, one of my key associates, I said to him, "Andy, I don't know what to do. We don't know what to do. If you were in my shoes, how would you reorganize this church?"

Andy has been a part of our senior leadership for five years, and to my surprise he said to me, "Nobody has ever actually asked me to think like that." But think like that he did. A week later he handed me a six-page, single-spaced proposal. I confess I was a little intimidated. When you ask a man for his counsel, he might actually tell you what he thinks. Andy did. And God spoke.

Although we have not adopted every little suggestion in his proposal, Andy did, in fact, put his finger on the key issue. Somehow God enabled him to see the problem and then to express what he saw with extraordinary clarity. And I couldn't see it until Andy showed me. Now everyone on our senior team would say that we have never experienced such a unity of purpose, and our church is now ready to leap into the future.

What Do You Think?

Church leaders are, I fear, more often not likely to be so open, so willing to welcome counsel and correction. A few years ago I was asked to mediate a serious church crisis that became a war between pastor and elders. Ever hear of one of those before? I don't have words to describe my stunned perplexity when one of the "offending elders" said to me, with tears in his eyes, "I've been a close friend with my pastor for more than ten years, but *never*, not on one occasion, has he asked me, 'What do you think?'"

"Never *once?*" I replied in disbelief.

"No, not once," he repeated.

Wait a minute. Wasn't I that way in the first half of my ministry? Didn't I think that just about every misunderstanding was somebody else's fault? After all, I'm such a good communicator. I have a huge church, and when I speak, all those people just sit there reverently, hanging on every word I say. If I have a disgruntled elder, what's that blip on the huge radar screen of my success? I was out of touch with what leadership guru Warren Bennis said: "The higher you go in leadership, the greater your influence, the harder it is for people to say no to you."

This is why Jesus had to stand in the middle of my road to Damascus and shine his piercing light on all my highly sophisticated, success-affirmed denial systems. And this leads me right into the story of Jacob, a very good guy from a very good family with a very good future. How would you like to say your grandfather was Abraham, your father Isaac?

Everything Jacob did, it seemed, turned to gold, and just about everybody would have said it was the blessing of God. Like me, Jacob had essentially no "testimony." Sure, he had done a few devious things—offended his father, his brother, his uncle—but then don't we all weasel our way in and out of some of the more difficult situations in life?

Yes, we do. It's the Jacob in all of us. Jacob, you probably know, is a Hebrew word that means literally "the one who grasps the heel," because he was born hanging on to his "older" brother Esau's foot. Figuratively, Jacob means "deceiver." Jacob was a really good guy, spiritual and successful too, but he was out of touch with the pain he caused for virtually everyone in his family. For those of you who may not be familiar with the whole Jacob narrative, I've summarized it here for you.

■ What Tangled Webs We Weave

- Genesis 27: Jacob, a name that means "deceiver," deceives his father and steals his brother Esau's blessing.
- Genesis 28: Jacob runs away from home because his brother intends to kill him, and on the way to his Uncle Laban's home, he has his famous dream at Bethel of angels ascending and descending on the ladder of God: "I will come back and build you a house here," Jacob promises God, *"If you bless me."* Such a deal!
- Genesis 29: Jacob, the sly man of the Middle East, is welcomed into the home of the number two sly man of the Middle East, Laban, his uncle. After Jacob works seven years to marry the love of his life, Rachel, Laban tricks him on his wedding night into marrying Rachel's ugly older sister, Leah. How that exactly happened is anybody's guess.
- Genesis 31: In the middle of one dark desert night, sly Jacob packs up and leaves Uncle Laban's land. He is accompanied by his sweet, tricky wife, who steals her father's

"family gods." See how she deceives her father in verses 34–35.

The narrative culminates in Genesis 32, both the high point and the low point of Jacob's life. Sent to let Esau know his hated brother was coming home, messengers raced back to Jacob and warned him, "We went to your brother Esau, and now he is coming to meet you, and four hundred men are with him" (Gen. 32:6). Jacob feared that Esau was preparing not to welcome him, but to kill him.

■ Nobody but God

"So Jacob was left alone" (Gen. 32:24), which suggests so much more than simply the absence of other people. That night at a place near the Jabbok River, Jacob came to the end of himself. It was the place of God's choosing. He was right where God wanted him, right where God wants each of us, because only in our moments of greatest personal helplessness do we begin to discover the life-changing presence and power of God. As we have noted several times already in this book, God's strength is made perfect in our weakness. More of me necessarily means less of God, while less of me opens the door for more of God in my life.

Desperate in his utter helplessness, thinking that perhaps he was facing the end of his life, Jacob had nowhere else to go but into the presence of God. Out of options and out of tricks, Jacob spent the better part of the night wrestling with a mysterious stranger. Many have seen this as a biblical example of "the dark night of the soul," one of those life seasons of profound personal loss and despair, a time when we are painfully alone and even God, it seems, is against us.

Instead, we find that God is with us and for us. As dawn was breaking, a metaphor for Jacob's new life, the mysterious stranger said, "Let me go, for it is daybreak" (Gen. 32:26).

But Jacob replied, "I will not let you go unless you bless me."

The man asked him, "What is your name?"

"Jacob," he answered.

Then the man said, "Your name will no longer be Jacob, but Israel, because you have struggled with God and with men and have overcome."

Jacob said, "Please tell me your name."

But he replied, "Why do you ask my name?" Then he blessed him there.

So Jacob called the place Peniel, saying, "It is because I saw God face to face, and yet my life was spared."

Genesis 32:26–30

■ Facing God, Face to Face with Yourself

I know that what I'm about to say is not specifically stated in the text of Genesis 32, but Jacob, I believe, was not only wrestling with the angel of the Lord, he was also wrestling with himself. As he came to the end of himself, something about him was about to change forever. As Jacob grappled with the mysterious stranger on that dark and lonely night, something popped—his hip. And for the rest of his life, he walked with a limp.

I have a limp. My heart limps. Doctors call it an arrhythmia. Every time my heart skips a beat (it still happens now and then, and I can still feel the irregularity), God reminds me that my life is marked. From time to time I still wrestle with God, but somehow it has become much easier to let go. Wrestling with God weakens my selfish resolve to protect my identity at all costs. The pain of life has loosened the death-grip of self-reliance. Goleman writes:

> In building leadership, sudden, shocking discoveries about our lives may shake us into action, "wowing" us with a stark truth about ourselves and offering new clarity about our lives. Such startling discontinuities can be frightening or enlightening. Some people react by running from them. Some simply deny their power and shrug them off. Others hear the wake up call,

sharpen their resolve, and start to transform self-defeating habits into new strengths.[7]

■ So What about You?

Okay, so I've bared my soul. Are you making judgments about me? Are you thinking, "That brother needs help!"

Or may I intrude into *your* life for a moment. What about you? Do you know yourself, really? The answer to that question should be an unequivocal, "No, I don't really know myself." I know it hurts to hear this, but if you think you really know what you're like, you don't. You're in denial.

Perhaps this is a better question: Do you have a network of peer mentors to whom you have given full permission to speak into your life? I don't just mean a circle of important people in ministry you hang with. Let me ask again: Do you have a network of peer mentoring relationships to which you are committed for the rest of your life? If you can't say yes, then you probably don't know yourself.

Bill Hybels writes:

> I have learned over the years that I am not strong enough to face the rigors of church work alone. In addition to the support of my wife and kids, I need the support of close friends. I need a small circle of trusted brothers and sisters with whom I can discuss temptations lest I fall to them. I need a few safe people with whom I can process feelings of frustration so that I don't become emotionally toxic. I need a few people in my life who will reflect grace back to me when I foul up and feel unusable. It's a powerful thing to receive grace from fellow human beings.[8]

In chapter 5 we read that Stanley and Clinton found that leaders who failed to reach full maturity and didn't finish well did not have a significant relational network or cut themselves off from their network as they grew older. Thus, these prominent leaders of leaders wrote: "We have personally determined that we will develop and maintain an active relational network for ourselves and pay whatever cost is necessary to do it."[9]

Al and I have personally discovered the importance, indeed, the *necessity,* of relational networks because, as the title of this chapter certainly suggests, "Al saved my life." Our hope and prayer for you is that like Paul Stanley and Robert Clinton, you will make every effort, at "whatever cost," to invest your time and energy in friendships for life. Leadership in any setting is no easy task. As Jesus himself taught us, "From everyone who has been given much, much will be demanded; and from the one who has been entrusted with much, much more will be asked" (Luke 12:48). The stakes are high, and those who have the special and rare gift of leadership *must* nurture and protect that gift in a circle of trusted friends.

Friendships for Life

"It is not good for . . . man to be alone."

—God

I (Gary) found the following findings startling.

> Whereas three or more incidents of intense stress within a year
> (say serious financial trouble, being fired, or a divorce) triple
> the death rate in socially isolated middle-aged men, *they have
> no impact whatsoever on the death rate of men who cultivate
> many close relationships.*[1]

At least in this study, researchers found that friendship literally keeps you alive when everything inside you wants to die. A lot of people exercise regularly and watch their fat intake religiously. Some take an aspirin every day to help prevent a heart attack. But cultivate friendships? Who could have imagined?

Maybe God, who said to himself, "It is not good for . . . man to be alone." A year ago a pastor friend of mine in Tucson, Roger Barrier, pointed out to me that God made this declara-

107

tion *before* Adam and Eve fell into sin. In other words, in God's perfect world, something still wasn't just right: man was alone, and that was not good.

Earlier we highlighted a similar negativity: 70 percent of the pastors in North America do not have anyone they consider a very close friend—and the number is even higher for their spouses. We don't have the research to prove it, but it seems likely that this is one of the primary causes of failure in ministry, and as we noted earlier, of an estimated fifteen hundred pastors resigning monthly.

■ A Journey into Covenant Friendships

I have had four milestones on the footpath of my journey into deeper, more significant relationships, but before I tell you where I've been, you need to know who I am. Like most pastors, it seems, I have two dissimilar sides to my personality. Some people might call it a split personality, but it's not really. You see, we pastors have an extraordinarily public life. Like politicians, we're out there pressing the flesh and kissing babies. People see us energized by preaching and teaching, and most of us have learned how to be fairly comfortable in social settings. So to most of the people in my life, I seem outgoing and gregarious. The other side of me, though, is very private. I think I even have some introvert blood in me. I like traveling alone and being alone.

■ Too Many "Friends"

As every pastor knows, men and women in Christian ministry, no matter how social, have so many people in their lives that they *learn* to like being alone. And, of course, all those people whom God has called you to lead along the journey of discipleship and transformation end up telling you how you're supposed to change. Pastors are always just a closed door away from countless people, many of whom are just a breath away from speaking into their pastor's life.

So who needs more friends in a world like that?

Therein lies the problem. All of us know that crowds of people don't morph into multiple deep friendships. In fact, being around many people prevents the development of significant relationships with just a few. A man or woman with many friends probably has no close friends. Significant relationships must be cultivated.

Jesus understood that. Overwhelmed by the multitudes who gathered to receive his ministry, he devoted himself to just a handful of very personal friends, twelve to be exact; and of those twelve, Peter, James, and John seem to have been his very closest companions. Surprisingly, the Bible says nothing about people being upset because they were outside Jesus' circle of close friends. Nevertheless, this is another of those unrealistic expectations for pastors. God loves everybody the same, we are told, which translated means, "Pastor, you shouldn't have any favorite people in your church. We all love you, and you should love us all the same," which means equal time for everyone. So everyone is my friend and no one is my good friend.

A few years ago I received an unusually angry fifteen-page letter. It was so nasty I had to have one of my associates read it and summarize the concerns for me. Because this person had a fairly prominent and influential role in our large church, I couldn't just ignore the letter. So I took the high road and made every effort to resolve his concerns, one of which was that I had not allowed him into my "circle of friends." *That*, I told him kindly, would never happen, not because I didn't like him, but because I have deep friendships that I have cultivated for many years, and adding more people to the social lists of my life would be unhealthy for me. He and his family left the church.

■ Milestone #1: Ray Anderson

As I mentioned earlier, four "events" have shaped my understanding of the necessity of cultivating long-term friendships.

The first was, of all things, a seminary class taught by Dr. Ray Anderson. A professor of systematics at Fuller Seminary, his specialty was the life and theology of Dietrich Bonhoeffer, the German pastor and author of the classic book *The Cost of Discipleship*. A devotional study of the Sermon on the Mount, *The Cost of Discipleship* was written in the crucible of intense community, when in reaction to the partnership of the state church with Adolf Hitler, Bonhoeffer founded his Confessing Church.

Probably more than any other subject, the church was near to Bonhoeffer's heart, which led him to write another lesser-known book, *Life Together*, a short treatise on the theology and practice of Christian community. It has touched me deeply. As you may know, Bonhoeffer was executed in a Nazi camp just four days before the end of World War II.

It was, as I remember, in one of Ray Anderson's classes that I understood for the first time—even though I had been in full-time Christian work for more than ten years—that relationship with God and relationships in the Christian community are inseparable. As John teaches in his first epistle, to love God is to love one another, and to love one another is to love God.

We Protestants tend to put a premium on things like doctrine and the priesthood of every believer, often at the expense of relationship and community. "Fundamentalists love God and hate people," I was told by one of my less conservative friends. The clear message of 1 Corinthians 13, however, is that if I am

spiritually gifted ("If I speak in the tongues of men and of angels"),

theologically astute ("If I have the gift of prophecy and can fathom all mysteries and all knowledge"),

full of miracle-working faith ("If I have a faith that can move mountains"),

generous to a fault ("If I give all I possess to the poor"), and

---

A Simple Theology of Community

- God is uncommon, unconditional love. The Triune God of the Bible is the prototypical community; that is, God is in himself community: three interdependent persons interfacing freely and fully with one another in *being* (who God is in his nature), in *purpose* (what God intends), and in *practice* (what God does). (See Genesis 1:26.)
- God created us in his image to reflect that image, that is, to live together in a community of interdependent relationships and uncommon love. (See Genesis 1:26–27.)
- Unbounded relationship with God and one another ("The man and his wife were both naked, and they felt no shame," Gen. 2:25) was lost when Adam and Eve fell into sin. Subsequently, human persons have been hiding from God, from one another, and from the truth about themselves, all the while desperately trying to find their identity apart from God and apart from one another. Individuality, though, does not exist outside of community. To be fully me, I need you.
- The work of Christ restores God's image in us through the church. (See Ephesians 2:13–16.) The church is the people of God living in a community of uncommon, unbounded love, offering to others the uncommon, unbounded love they are desperately seeking for themselves apart from God.

---

willing to die for Christ ("If I surrender my body to the flames"),

"but have not love, I gain nothing." The greatest of all is love, because God is love.

Community? What's That?

Sadly, I've found that the importance of the church to God is lost on many of us fiercely independent North American Christians. In searching to know and experience God's love for me, I look right past God's love for the church, even though his Son,

Jesus, "gave himself up for her to make her holy . . . to present her to himself as a radiant church" (Eph. 5:25–27).

In fact, I've come to believe that community (*koinonia*, shared-life) is the single most difficult biblical construct for American Christians to understand, because it is radically countercultural to the American ideals of privacy and personal freedom.

In his book *We the Lonely People,* Ralph Keyes wrote:

> "Community" is a national obsession. *But we want other things more.* Not getting involved with the neighbors is worth more to us than "community." . . . It's this confusion, this ambivalence, that confounds our quest for community. We yearn for a simpler, more communal life; we sincerely want more sense of community. But not at the sacrifice of any advantages that mass society has brought, even ones we presumably scorn.[2]

We want other things more? Like what? Why are community and lasting relationships collapsing in America? Why are we such lonely people? Robert Putnam did extensive social research for his landmark book *Bowling Alone*[3] and discovered numerous enemies of friendship and community. The primary enemies are discussed here.

Restlessness. Way back in 1849, a Scottish journalist by the name of Alexander McKay wrote, "How readily an American makes up his mind to try his fortunes elsewhere." Called the "M-factor"—movement, migration, and mobility—it is what has shaped our national character and our Christianity. As Americans we have even found that there is a direct relationship between mobility and success. You have to move to get a better job. Even clergy do that.

Mobility, though, is an enemy of friendship. As a direct result of our freedom of movement, we Americans have learned how to make friends quickly—and leave them behind just as quickly. Putnam writes, "People who expect to move in the next five years are 20–25 percent less likely to attend church, . . . volunteer, or work on community projects than those who expect to stay put."[4]

Technology, mass media, and mostly TV. What I read in *Bowling Alone* about the impact of TV blew me away. In fact, I think I've found the devil! He has a big cubic head, and whenever you see his face, it's always just on the other side of a large glass surface on the front of that cube. *Television!* Studies have found that watching it is literally a mindless activity, because it has a measurable mesmerizing effect on the human brain.

According to Putnam, television absorbed 40 percent of the average American's free time in 1995. In the previous thirty years, we Americans gained an average of six hours a week in leisure time, but we spent almost all six of those additional hours watching TV. As someone has said, "Television is the eight-hundred-pound gorilla of leisure time."

Putnam tells us what television will do to undermine relationships in our homes and communities.

- Husbands and wives spend three to four times as much time watching TV together as they spend talking to each other.
- Couples spend six to seven times more time watching TV than participating in church and community activities outside their home.
- More and more of our TV viewing is alone, with less than 5 percent of teens watching with their parents.
- In the evening Americans, *above all else,* watch TV. And the percent of Americans watching TV is much higher than the percent of those talking with their families.
- The more people watch TV, the less they volunteer, write letters to friends and family, participate in clubs and group activities, attend church, and feel good about themselves.[5]

Television steals our humanity and deprives us of community. Like busyness and mobility, television prevents us from cultivating significant relationships with family and friends. But there's one more enemy of community:

Materialism. Television is, essentially, a Trojan horse of advertising. Practically speaking, the entertainment element is only a vehicle to carry advertisements into your home. Ads, in turn, are cleverly designed to create a sense of need, discontent, and restlessness. The intentional message of all advertising is that whatever you have, it's not enough—a decidedly nonbiblical state of mind.

Not Restless in Russia

Just six months ago my brother Dave and his wife Tonya adopted two Russian orphans, Nicholas (thirteen) and Natasha (seven). Those kids came to the States with literally nothing but the clothes on their bodies. Naturally, my brother wanted to bless them. Every red-blooded American kid has to have at least three things: a bike, Rollerblades, and video games. So that's what Nicholas got, but to my brother's dismay, he found that the more he gave Nick, the more unruly he became. Nick's relationship with his new mom and dad, who had sacrificed so much to give him and his little sister a new life, became less important than his stuff. So Dave took it all away, boxed it up, and put it in storage. And an amazing thing happened. Nick, my brother said, became peaceful, compliant, and happy.

"It's an indictment of our society," I observed.

"Absolutely," my brother replied. "I've thought deeply about that, how 'things' disrupt our lives by interfering in our relationship with God and others, and Nicholas is a prime example."

"What good is it for a man to gain the whole world," Jesus said, "and yet lose or forfeit his very self?" (Luke 9:25). Our restless obsession with self-gratification through possessions and entertainment leaves us little time for God or for one another.

"Social Capital"

On the other hand, in his huge national study Putnam found that in states where "social capital" is high, that is, where people cultivate community, the following things happen:

For Thought, Discussion, and Prayer

1. How do you understand community, koinonia, sharing life with others?
2. What is your theology of community?
3. From your perspective, how important do you think community is to God?
4. How do you view your own experience in community? Disconnected? Trying to connect? Immersed? How many people in your life would you consider close friends?
5. How often do you ask advice from other people you consider close to you?
6. Do you have a mentor, a spiritual guide? How often do you meet with a group of people to share personal needs and pray?
7. Where in your life are the barriers to deeper relationships with others?
8. What are some things you can do to cultivate meaningful friendships?

- kids are better off
- schools work better
- kids watch TV less
- violent crime is rarer
- hostility levels among citizens are lower
- people are more tolerant of one another
- public health is better
- mortality is lower[6]

The significance of this array of social research is that there are extraordinary benefits when we cultivate significant friendships and calamitous consequences when we don't.

■ Milestone #2: 1987

It was three years after 1984, but for me the year was still Orwellian. In the previous chapter, I wrote at length about my experiences and the lessons learned that year. My world fell apart. It was the worst of times, but it was also the best of times, because without the extraordinary stretching of my soul, I would not have understood myself or my need for significant, accountable relationships.

Although the theology of community became so very real to me through Ray Anderson's teaching (I told him at the end of one class that his sessions felt like revival meetings to me) I did not, could not perceive my own disconnect from genuine community. Yes, I had friends—some very good ones. And although I always had thought of myself as someone who listened to advice, God knew I had a long way to go.

Al, I suppose, was the first person to help me see my blindness (now that's an interesting concept), and because of my pain, I was as open to counsel as I ever had been. Transformation, though, did not come until I had an uncommon moment with God—at the same retreat center where I am, right now, writing this book.

I had come here to work first and pray later, but a little book in the literature rack jumped out at me: *Life in the Fast Lane* by Keith Miller. As I read his introduction about the defining moment when, on a treadmill, he discovered suddenly and violently that his life was on the brink of ending, I felt the Spirit of prayer fall on my soul unlike anything I have experienced before or since. I prayed and I wept and I listened. God, though, was doing most of the speaking.

Somewhat like a near-death experience, one relationship problem in my life after another paraded through my mind, and I saw with brutal clarity the pain I had unwittingly and selfishly caused for so many people. Remarkably, although I felt profound conviction and grief in true repentance, I felt no guilt, no condemnation. In the same moment, with equal intensity, I experienced both the purging and the mercy of God in a foretaste of the judgment seat of Christ. Like Jacob at the Jabbok, I came face to face with God, face to face with myself.

That day I made a list of people whom I knew I had to ask for forgiveness. My wife came first. Then former staff. Others.

For Thought, Discussion, and Prayer

1. What are your two or three most significant life experiences and why?
2. In your moments of greatest pain, do you find yourself reaching for or running from God? From others? Why?
3. Over the next few weeks, in your quiet times with God, ask him to show you relationships in your life that need healing. Perhaps you need to ask a few people for forgiveness. Perhaps you need to talk with someone about how you can take the initiative, like Jesus did, to restore a broken relationship in your life.

It was a small, painful step for me, a giant leap for God and the important people in my life. God saw me bringing my gift to the altar and said, essentially, "I don't want your gift until you take the initiative to make things right with your brothers and sisters" (see Matt. 5:23–24).

■ Milestone #3: Early Morning Men's Prayer

When you hear the word *cultivate,* what comes to your mind? Here are some synonyms that pop up in my cyberspace thesaurus: develop, enrich, grow, improve, nurture, produce, promote.

To me, all these words have one thing in common: initiative. You have to take it, or it won't happen. Cultivating friendships is like investing in the stock market. Long-term, over many years, even decades, your investments will reward you handsomely. You know, of course, that there are many risks, but no one just puts his or her money in a hole in the ground. Well, one guy did, in a parable Jesus told about giving back what God gives you. The master "called his servants and entrusted his property to them" (Matt. 25:14). Two of the servants took the risk and invested the entrusted talents well. They were the faithful ones, Jesus said. A third was afraid and buried his in the backyard. Not good.

And it is not good for man to be alone. Our sin and shame, however, are enormous obstacles on the road back to God and others, and though salvation is by grace alone, it is not, as Dietrich Bonhoeffer termed it, "cheap grace." Certainly, God works in us "to will and to act according to his good purpose," but "my dear friends, as you have always obeyed . . . continue to *work out your salvation with fear and trembling"* (Phil. 2:12–13, italics mine).

Walking with God is serious business, and after you get saved, there is nothing more important to God than your relationships with others: "Love God with all you've got," commanded Jesus, "And when you've done that, love your neighbor." In other words, friendships—something God very much wants in your life—don't just happen. You have to cultivate them.

Spiritual leaders aren't always so spiritual. Sometimes we even let whole days go by without a single focused prayer. To cultivate more disciplined prayer in my life, I decided I would create a set time and specific place for men to pray. I admit the idea wasn't original with me. It came from an *Injoy* teaching tape on which John Maxwell—still a pastor at the time—spoke about his own men's prayer meeting—held at 5:30 in the morning!

One by one I personally invited men—sometimes with their wives standing right there listening—to join me. How could they refuse? After less than a year, we had about fifty men gathering every Wednesday morning for an hour of worship, Bible study, and small group prayer. Fifteen years later we're still doing it. Want to know our secret? Two simple rules: You have to be there every week unless you're sick or out of town, and you have to make a commitment for six months.

I take attendance and follow up persistently with those who are AWOL. Our expectation is for the guys to be hot or cold, in or out. My relentless insistence on commitment has offended a few of the men, because this is a "free country," but I happily remind them that we told them "the rules" the first day they showed up. My intent for our meeting has been to pray, but more than that, to create a place where we are intentional about cultivating prayer and relationships.

Some of the men have been in our early morning prayer and commitment groups for more than ten years. I asked Ray Jensen, an associate vice president at Arizona State University and a member of our governing board at Word of Grace, to tell you briefly why our sunrise prayer has had such an impact on his life.

> It's been over ten years since I stepped into a relationship with three other men that centers on Gary's weekly men's prayer meeting. It's been years since the idea of staying in bed has been more than a fleeting thought.
>
> Each week, the four of us open our lives to one another. My friends are now familiar with my deepest needs, fears, hopes, and dreams. They have walked with me as I have staggered or failed in relationships. They have comforted me when I have been wounded or disappointed. They have challenged me to live at a higher level, to step into opportunities, to heal broken relationships, and to risk new relationships. They know me so well that I wouldn't make a major employment or relational decision without seeking their counsel.
>
> Like any deep relationship, ours did not develop quickly. It has grown one conversation, one prayer, one breakfast at a time. We laugh about the fact that it can be easier to confess our failings to God than to have to face each other. One of my favorite portions of Scripture is when Jesus tells us that we won't really see him until we see those who come in his name. Each week I meet with my three friends and brothers. They come in his name, reflecting his grace, and in them I see Jesus.

The lesson here is that prayer—and relationships—don't just happen. We have to take the initiative to make them happen, and they have to be cultivated. God is working in us, but we have to work out our salvation with fear and trembling. But, then, it's probably much easier just to sit down in front of the television and do nothing.

For Thought, Discussion, and Prayer

1. What are your God-given talents? With what property has God entrusted you? Think about that in terms of skills, resources, time, and meaningful relationships.
2. What are some things you might do to invest your "talents" more intentionally, more purposefully, and more effectively?
3. What are some specific things you might be able to do to invest in and cultivate two or three important relationships?

■ Milestone #4: Pastors in Covenant

Getting together with other Christian leaders has always energized me. When I was much younger I was both puzzled and troubled by pastors who made little or no effort to connect with other pastors. Just a few weeks ago I talked several friends and my wife, Marilyn, into traveling to Hagerstown, Maryland, for the 140th anniversary reenactment of the battle of Antietam, the bloodiest day in the American Civil War.

Standing shoulder to shoulder in a crowd of about forty thousand people waiting an hour or more to watch fifteen thousand reenactors is an opportunity to cultivate friendships with strangers! To my delight, the gentleman standing next to me was a pastor of a small country church just a few miles away.

I asked him a dozen or more questions about his ministry, his church, and the challenges of his unique calling to rural America. Genuinely friendly, he was particularly enthusiastic about their small but brand-new facility. I was disappointed to find out, though, that when I asked him about what else God was doing in his area, he knew little or nothing about the other churches in his community. In fact, he didn't ask me a single question about what I was doing. Nothing.

From Acquaintance to True Friend

My dear friend Hal Sacks shares my passion for bringing pastors together. Founders of BridgeBuilders, a ministry to ministers, Hal and his wife, Cheryl, have championed and cultivated spiritual unity, ministry partnerships, and prayer in the Phoenix metro area for two decades. For years the Sacks organized monthly citywide ministers' lunches featuring some of the best-known Christian leaders in America, including such diverse notables as Jack Hayford, John Maxwell, Bill Bright, and Oral Roberts.

I attended those luncheons regularly, yes, to hear the great speakers, but mostly because I enjoyed getting together with other men and women of God in a setting of denominational and ethnic diversity. Without the lunches, most of us would have seen each other rarely, but with them some of us became friends.

Sharing similar challenges and recognizing a need to spend time with one another, a dozen or so of us leaders of "independent" churches decided to get together monthly for our own fellowship lunch. It was great for about six months, but keeping our commitment to get together was not high on our list of priorities. You know, we were all so busy—and probably watching television too.

I can't remember who said it first, but one of us called everyone's attention to the insignificance of our friendships, betrayed by irregular attendance at our gatherings and evidenced by our marginal devotion to one another. All of us sensed that God was challenging us to a deeper level of relationship, but we had no idea what that might mean. So we agreed, for starters, that we would go to a retreat center together to dialogue and pray about why we liked each other and what that could possibly mean for each of us and our churches.

Pastors in Covenant

One retreat led to another, and in the summer of 1997 we spent three days at a hot Arizona desert resort identifying our core values and developing a relationship covenant, *writing it down and signing it*. Here are some of the things we discussed:

Covenant. Not rules, but boundaries. As much as we independent pastors resisted "institutionalizing" our mini-movement, we did agree that we needed to define in the simplest terms what it meant to be in relationship with one another. We decided that the kind of relationship with one another we were longing for required a commitment to regular meetings of a closed group for an extended period of time.

So we resolved to meet monthly for three hours rather than an hour a week, because it takes quality time to talk and pray. We also determined that we would expect one another to make attendance at our meeting a personal calendar priority by scheduling other ministry demands around our covenant meeting.

Anyone who missed more than three meetings a year, we said, would risk forfeiting his or her place in the group, a simple commitment that has had dramatic effect on the faithfulness of group members. To say we were friends was one thing. It has been quite another to insist that each of us show up on time at virtually every meeting. In a sense this nine-out-of-twelve rule emerged from the attendance expectations of my sunrise men's prayer meeting, which by then had sustained itself for nearly ten years.

"Having a monthly meeting and spending time caring and sharing with each other as friends slowly erodes a sense of isolation that is often part of being a senior pastor," says my friend Keith Andrews, senior pastor of St. James Episcopal Church and a participant in one of my groups. "And when my congregation hears me talk about other pastors and about the caring relationships," he adds, "there is more of a cooperative effort in the congregation to care about those in other churches."

Accountability. Simply, we agreed to submit to one another, but like everything else, that had to be defined as well—*and written down*. We identified three areas to which we would hold one another accountable: (1) doctrine, (2) professional conduct, and (3) personal behavior. But how do you define those three things?

After no little discussion, we determined to keep it simple. For doctrine, we decided to use as our standard the Apostles' Creed, a giant leap for a roomful of independent church pastors. We agreed on the creed, though, because we had a prophetic sense that our group would become a model for many other groups. For professional conduct and personal behavior, we said we would abide by the teaching of the Pastoral Epistles.

We also agreed that participation in our group would not preclude involvement in other networks and/or associations. We do, however, submit to one another as defined by our covenant. No, we don't monitor one another, but we are committed to building one another up. Keith Andrews wrote to me, "Joining a covenant group is not about getting busy with one more project. We're there to facilitate each other's growth, health, and leading with excellence."

Exclusivity. This was a tough one, but having worked so hard on the relationships in our group, we agreed that groups needed to be closed, that no one could invite someone else to become a part of the group unless everyone in the group agreed. In our first group, which has been meeting for more than six years, we have lost and gained only two people. Of those we lost, one left the ministry (we did everything we could to help him process that) and the other started his own covenant group.

More Groups Than We Could Have Imagined

Dan Davis, pastor to pastors in Austin, Texas, and a pastor to me personally, attended our milestone retreat and helped us facilitate the development of our covenant. Having a heart and passion for leaders himself, Dan excitedly presented our "pastors in covenant" model to a number of his friends in Austin. Within just a couple of years, a dozen covenant groups, as diverse as the Christian community in Austin—and one interracial—were meeting in churches and homes from one end of the city to the other.

We have had an extraordinary response here in Phoenix too, as I took the initiative to cultivate the second of what has become a dozen or so groups in our area. Thinking evangelistically about intentional friendships, I felt that our first group was perhaps too monolithic, since all of us are about the same age and pastor very similar churches. If we had discovered something, then, like the wheel, it should have universal application.

So I invited three other leaders to join me in forming a second, more diverse group. John Vawter (former pastor and president of Western Conservative Baptist Seminary and first president of Phoenix Seminary), Bill Thrall (author of the best-selling book *The Ascent of a Leader*), Len Griffin (lifelong friend, pastor, and participant in our first group), and I agreed that each of us would pray about inviting a friend to help us start our second group.

For that second group, our first year was really bumpy. We weren't cultivating; we were plowing up a stony field! Our diversity was a challenge, for our group included:

the pastor of a seeker church
a Nazarene church pastor
a seeker Nazarene church pastor
two charismatic pastors
the pastor of a Christian church
an Episcopal priest
the pastor of a Bible church

But four years, more than fifty meetings, and four three-day retreats later, our time together has become three of the most treasured hours of each month. Those guys are my friends! After four years, though, we are still asking basic questions like, What does this group mean? Why are we meeting? How do we go deeper?

Like the farmer who replants his field every spring, we keep cultivating. All of us are deeply committed to the process, and

---

For Thought, Discussion, and Prayer

1. Do you have a group of trusted friends you meet with regularly?
2. Do you and your spouse have a group of trusted couples you meet with regularly?
3. Is your spouse getting the support he or she needs from close friends?
4. Are leaders in your church cultivating significant, mentoring relationships? In what ways do you think your church or ministry would be healthier and more effective if they did?
5. Do you have a reasonably close friend or two who might be interested in exploring a commitment to one another to cultivate your relationship? Is this something you feel the leading of God about? Why? Why not?

---

for every one of us, our group has been a safe refuge—a place of support, counsel, and healing in difficult times.

■ Jesus Cultivated Friendships for Life

Let's wrap up this chapter with a few thoughts about friendship with the one we serve. In John 15:14–15 Jesus said, "You are my friends if you do what I command. I no longer call you servants, because a servant does not know his master's business. Instead, I have called you friends, for everything that I learned from my Father I have made known to you."

"Instead" means something new is happening, and in the context of John 15, it is radical. God in Christ is giving birth to the new covenant! The rules and times *are* changing. "I *no longer* call you servants. *Instead,* I have called you *friends.*" No, we're not servants anymore, bound by tasks and rules. God wants us to be his *friends!* And he demonstrated that by becoming one of us in the person of his Son, Jesus. Our walk with God is meant to be love-based, relationship-based, not task-driven.

"What I have learned from my Father I have made known to you." Ministry is learned primarily in the context of deep, personal mentoring relationships. Not in books. Not at conferences. Not even in the stimulating discussions of ministers' meetings and leadership networks.

And Jesus said that "friends . . . do what I command." Commands are written down. In other words, friendship is not just about all the great feelings you share with someone who is special in your life. Good fences make good neighbors, and good boundaries make for lasting and productive friendships—with God and with one another.

How Our Group Works

There are a lot of conferences and books on leadership skills, theology, organizational development. . . . But what I value here is being able to talk to you guys about things I'm dealing with on a personal level and finding that someone has already dealt with these same issues. I get the benefit of all your experience.

—Pastors in Covenant group member

Success in ministry isn't just about knowledge, spirituality, vision, and leadership skill. Gary and I think it is also about emotional maturity, and part of that is connectedness with others. Pastors who excel in ministry recognize that they must be continually nourished, refined, and renewed with other people who are like they are.

Effective pastors have to address colliding expectations and shifting demands in ministry. They must balance self-care with service to the congregation, community, and their families. To do this effectively requires sustenance, support, and continual growth and change. As Gary has explained, growth and change come through the application of God's wisdom and truth in the day-to-day experiences, difficulties, and crises of life—as we are encouraged and coached by peers, mentors, advisors, and friends who understand. This is why we believe that God is calling pastors and other ministry leaders into a new leadership model that requires transformational covenant friendships.

■ Let's Do *More Than* Lunch

What we are proposing, however, is a leap beyond ministers' luncheons and prayer summits. Those kinds of things are both important and indispensable, but working together—or even praying together regularly—does not necessarily allow us to do the kind of relationship work that is so desperately needed for leaders to last.

If your experience is like ours, you probably have become acquainted with other pastors and ministry executives in your area as a result of some event or task. It may have been something as basic and as vital as prayer, but it was a task nevertheless. Regardless of what denomination we belong to and how many apostolic networks and kingdom partnerships we form or are a part of, we leaders continue to dance and court without ever really making a serious commitment to one another to be long-term, accountable friends.

■ All Kinds of Leaders Need Support

My brother-in-law, Lynn, and I (Al) were riding down the cart path of the third hole of a beautiful desert golf course in Scottsdale, Arizona. A successful businessman, Lynn has survived multiple business transitions and crises and a few family ones too. Knowing that he had once gone to therapy himself and that his wife is a therapist, I was wondering what he would say when I asked him, "With the difficult things you've gone through, what has helped you the most in life?"

"My TEC friends," was his immediate answer.

I kind of expected him to say, "My wife," or, in jest, "Therapy." But no, he said it was his friends who stood by him and helped him through life. Are you a pastor? A Christian leader? How would you have answered my question? Would you have given me a more "spiritual" response, like, "God sustained me"? Or, "The Bible"? Obviously, the foundation for wholeness in Christian ministry is our relationship with God and his Word! But if you are a leader, do you have significant friendships?

Lynn belonged to a TEC group for eighteen years. TEC is an acronym for The Executive Committee. Owned by Michael Milken, TEC is a program specifically designed for top business executives to ensure their long-term success. It's based on the knowledge that "it's lonely at the top," and therefore high-profile executives need peer relationships. TEC members meet once a month for a full day, the morning session for a relevant business presentation and the afternoon session for personal sharing. Lynn told me, "My TEC friends helped me through the hard business times and also through the personal crises. I wouldn't have made it without them. Since I've sold my business, I am no longer in TEC, but those guys are still my friends. We get together for lunch at least once a month."

Isolation isn't endemic to ministry leadership alone; it happens to all kinds of leaders. TEC is a profitable company that charges members dues of more than a thousand dollars a month. Business leaders gladly pay it—because it works! It helps make them successful. TEC cultivates leaders who last.

■ Intentionality—A Core Value

Our Pastors in Covenant (PIC) model is similar to TEC. We didn't design it that way; it just evolved naturally. Both, though, have much in common. For example, being intentional about relationships is a major core value for us. Pastors are busy; business executives are busy. Demands of the day often exceed the time limits of the day. If, however, we are too busy to have friends, we are simply too busy.

When husbands, for example, come to me for counsel on how to pay more attention to their wives, I tell them, "Just put it into your schedule!" I learned early that if Susan, my wife, was on my schedule for lunch Friday, I would end up meeting with her and enjoying our time together. But if I didn't schedule it, something always seemed to come up. Every little pressure and crisis seemed to take precedent, and we'd rarely end up meeting for lunch. It's what some have called "the tyranny of the urgent."

Our good friend Hal Sacks has pioneered a bridge-building ministry for ministers in Arizona and has been influential around the country in getting Christian leaders together. After years of experience he says:

> Relationship must be intentional. We are called to something we know nothing about and yet we preach about—relationship with God, your family, and the world around you. After years of working with Christian leaders, I've come to realize that relationships are the most important issue and the most elusive. I've brought men together to pray assuming that prayer together would cultivate intimacy, but that in fact doesn't happen.

Someone once said that the road to hell is paved with good intentions. Likewise, the road to failure in ministry is paved with good intentions. Pastors know so much more than they can ever practice. Most will agree that they need meaningful relationships with peers. Few, however, take the simple step of making and scheduling time for them.

I like our PIC model because it is an easy way to schedule needed relationship. And it is okay to schedule relationship. Those who are more relational connect easily with others, while some find connecting difficult. To form a peer friendship, however, one need not be highly relational, only intentional and consistent about scheduling time with peers to talk and pray.

■ PIC Group Meetings

Since understanding how a PIC group works may help you become more committed to relationship, I will tell you about our prototype PIC group. Dan Scott is the pastor of Valley Cathedral in Phoenix. We meet monthly at his church on North Central Avenue. He has a small, well-lit, yet secluded cottage in his church's prayer garden. It is just right for us, because it is centrally located and private. Moreover, Dan's staff always provides a very nice spread of refreshments. We meet from 9 A.M. until noon on the first Thursday of every month. A few of us are always on time and a few are often late, but no one gets too upset about others not being punctual. As Gary has often said, "I have to 'perform' everywhere I go. This is one place I can just be myself."

I (Al) am currently the group facilitator, meaning that my role is to make sure everyone in our group gets a turn to share. This is a challenge when you're in the same room with seven other strong-willed Christian leaders who are often far more comfortable speaking than listening. Others have served as facilitator in the past; we share leadership. Mutual respect is another of our core values, and we believe that leadership of the group is a shared responsibility of all of its members working within their gifts and abilities.

We also think that a PIC group, whenever possible, should be comprised of the leaders of both large and small churches. In our PIC group we have a mixture of church sizes. We even have a couple of ministers who are not presently pastoring a church. For example, I am leading a ministry that assists churches. Another member pastors a thriving "upscale" church of over a thousand, while another pastors a small messianic congregation. Gary's interdenominational church has more than forty-five hundred attending every weekend. Another member, on the other hand, just left a church he founded to start a worldwide traveling ministry. One pastors a multiethnic congregation of several hundred, another is transitioning from a church to a parachurch ministry, and yet another is the second senior pastor of a one-thousand-member church that has been in crisis for several years. So, as you can see, our group is quite diverse. At eight participants, though, our group size is probably a little too large. When I share more about group dynamics, I will comment on how a smaller group size works better.

Our group meetings begin with informal dialogue between members. We spend time catching up on what has happened since the last meeting.

"Did you hear about. . . ?"

"Did you know that . . . is happening?"

These warmups are often followed by, "I read an interesting new book last week. . . ." Many group members enter into the discussion, others listen.

Our meetings seem inadvertently to follow the TEC meeting format my brother-in-law described. We usually start with "shoptalk" and conclude with sharing personal needs and concerns. The initial discussions often cover a wide range of subjects, from how to do worship services to the latest in church growth paradigms. We even get into local church politics on occasion.

Because our group members like to "preach," we've had to make a rule. Near the beginning of each meeting, somewhere in the middle of the shoptalk, I ask, "Who needs time today?" This ensures we don't miss the opportunity to hear and support a brother with a need. Second, we have committed to turn off the pastor babble by no later than 10:30 so that the remaining hour and a half can be focused entirely on personal issues. Most of the people in our group seem to feel more comfortable talking about ministry rather than personal issues. Once the sharing starts, however, all eyes are riveted on the person sharing his needs, and it is evident that everyone cares.

If no one needs immediate attention, we go around the room and check in. That means each of us shares a bit of what is happening in his personal life and ministry. Our sharing times over the years have been deeply personal and painful at times and joyful and hilarious at others. We've talked about everything:

- attraction to women other than our wives
- our marriages

- conflict with staff
- conflict with each other
- children on drugs
- children alienated from parents
- every kind of church problem
- personal doubts
- ministry failures, successes, and opportunities

We have tried to be as open with one another as we know how, and we have made our share of mistakes. Not infrequently we have to remind ourselves of the guidelines we have embraced to keep us on track. Here are the more important boundaries we have set for our meetings:

1. Whenever we open up the meeting to share what has been happening in our lives, the facilitator needs to ask, "Is there anyone here who needs time today?" With so many dominant personalities, we don't want to overlook someone's need.
2. After someone shares we will often ask, "Do you need counsel on this, or prayer, or both?" It is not always appropriate to give each other advice. Sometimes the best thing we can do for one another is to listen and pray.
3. We all agree to allow any of us to ask any of us any question about our personal or professional life, not rudely, of course, but gently and in the best interest of the one being asked the question. Without this openness there can be no real accountability and authenticity.
4. Occasionally, when we are spending time sharing personal needs, we break up into two or more smaller groups. We think this is helpful because the larger size of our group may at times complicate the group process.

Our group style fits us, but it isn't necessarily ideal for everyone. For example, Dan Davis and others in Austin, Texas, keep their groups smaller and in some cases will not allow shoptalk. Our other local PIC groups are also smaller. Some don't have

nearly as much interaction about ministry issues and prefer
to do things like read a book together and share its personal
application. Regardless of the individual group style and size,
though, all of us in PIC groups have embraced common core
values formed in the early stages of the formation of our first
pastor's groups. These are:

Relationship, Not Task

The core value that sustains us is treasuring relationship over
task. Maybe a better way to say it is that our goal is to develop
healthy viable peer friendships that will stand the test of time.
The primary purpose of a PIC group is not to engage in joint
kingdom partnerships or events. This happens, but it is not
our goal. Yes, we believe that healthy pastors leading healthy
churches change cities, and pastors and ministry leaders need
to join together in life-changing initiatives. We believe that
covenant groups, though, must remain relational in focus and
not become task- or initiative-driven. Dan Davis, the catalyst
for covenant groups in Austin, says it this way.

> A major purpose of these groups is to help us become more
> human. I have needed what Pastors in Covenant promotes: a
> safe place to be connected—with the assurance that this is not
> just another organizational solution. Coming together around
> tasks does not sustain relationships, but sustained relationships
> can lead to effective kingdom ventures.

Gary and I believe that when Christian leaders are committed
to forming healthy relationships with one another, cooperative
ministry will be the healthy outflow of those relationships.
Pastors are often entrepreneurial by nature. Many want to
do something together with other Christian leaders, but often
the missing element is the trust, personal commitment, and
close relationship needed to partner together in the work of
Christ.

George Barna tells us that only a percent or two of churches
in the same area ever work together, even when they have

shared vision. We believe that more partnerships are scuttled by mismanaged conflict, wrong expectations, suspicion, and lack of trust than from lack of vision. Relationship is a vehicle for purpose. One of our covenant brothers has struggled over the years with trying to bring churches together, but since joining a covenant group, things have changed. He says, "It's the friendships I've formed in my PIC group that have made it possible for us to sustain combined joint efforts to reach our community for Christ. It's also these long-term relationships that overcame the competition that existed."

Character Development

In attempting to define what we are trying to accomplish in our covenant groups, it was necessary for us to identify, understand, and embrace key core values. Godly character development is another one of those values. During one of our meetings, one of the guys shared about his background:

> I grew up in a pastor's home. When my father reached a point in his life when he was struggling in ministry, he had no one to go to. When he went to the guys in his denomination, they shamed him. So he left my mom and the ministry and has lived the last years of his life isolated from and hostile to the church. There was no place for him to deal with the inconsistencies of his life, so he just kept them hidden. I've seen that pastoral training and development is almost entirely information-driven, not character-based. Integrity is the gap between the way you ought to live and the way you actually live. Hypocrisy is acting like that gap doesn't exist.

There is a desperate need for authentic relationships in the body of Christ. When I (Al) work with ministries in helping them select new senior pastors or ministry leaders, I challenge them to look for three things:

1. *Calling.* Without a clear call from God there will not be the grace necessary to meet the extraordinary challenges

of Christian ministry. Grace for the task always comes with the call.

2. *Competence.* Look for the skills needed to fulfill the calling. If the job is primarily pulpit mastery and organizational envisioning, then make sure the person you select has these skills.

3. *Character.* Strength of personal character is the third foundation stone of a successful pastoral life.

Covenant group friendships cultivate good character development. When one of us is hurting and every emotion inside us wants to strike out, our close friends are the ones who help us bear the pain and respond rather than react. Responding to difficult, sinful people with a soft word, a conciliatory attitude, or a spoken apology demonstrates the character of Christ. We then become part of the solution rather than the problem. That's when we live out what we preach. Here is what a few covenant group members have shared about their character development.

> Through the intentional friendships I've developed with other pastors, I've discovered the God-given treasure of mature, godly friends, who speak into my life and refuse to let me drown in the swamp of my own self-interest. I couldn't have survived and thrived in ministry without their love and firm wisdom.
>
> The group has helped me become more transparent. Being transparent helps to overcome all the things that undermine my life and ministry—fear, insecurity, inhibitions, pride, anxiety, lack of training, my tendency to be overly controlling. . . .
>
> We leaders can only lead out of who we are. We can't lead effectively and do ministry out of concepts that are just ideas. Preaching is not where we fail. The subculture of the church is dysfunctional in proportion to the dysfunctions of its leaders. The church can never be anything more or less than who we are and how we act. The church will never change unless we repent of our artificiality, get real with ourselves and others, and change. My friends help me do just that.

Ten Character Assessment Questions

I (Al) borrowed the following idea from Bill Thrall's Leadership Catalyst Seminar partner Bruce McNicol. It's a list of key questions about character and conduct they use to evaluate whether or not a church leader is ready to participate in their leadership development program. I use their questions when interviewing candidates for ministry positions. How candidates answer them will tell the interviewer a lot about their character formation and relationships.

1. If you were losing objectivity, how would you reclaim it?
2. Whom do you trust? Whom are you willing to trust with you?
3. As you look over your shoulder, who is in the wake of your influence and how are they doing?
4. With whom do you intentionally share your needs? Which relationships have helped you mature?
5. Tell us two stories of times when you were in personal trauma, pain, or crisis and you trusted someone else to give you counsel and protection.
6. In what ways have you ignored advice that could have helped you?
7. Share two stories of when you paid the price for a choice of integrity, knowing that it could cost you reputation, a title or position, finances, or some other resource that was valuable to you.
8. Which of your life issues continue to surface to the extent that you need others to guard, guide, and protect you in those areas?
9. What challenges are you accepting for the benefit of those you are influencing?
10. What do you do to develop the kind of communities where integrity and character are nurtured?

Of course, no covenant group in itself can guarantee that a participant will develop godly character. What a group and

intentional covenantal relationships do, though, is provide a
context for growing in grace and character for those willing
to risk the adventure.

Other Core Values

Values are the things we esteem to be most important, the things
we live by, the truths that govern our priorities. Values, then, determine how we conduct ourselves with one another. Values are
what we live by, not just what we believe. Here are a few more we
think are important for covenant groups to be effective:

- *Dialogue.* Forums on various theological, leadership, and
  personal issues are important to fulfill the group's purpose
  of developing healthy leaders. We do this by both allowing
  and encouraging shared insights and knowledge among
  those of us in our group.
- *Availability.* The members of our group extend their
  commitment to be available to one another outside the
  schedule of our monthly meetings for developing friendships further or for providing personal counsel in times
  of difficulty or crisis.
- *Inclusivity.* We see the need for relationship among pastors
  of every denominational persuasion and ethnic group. It
  is healthy to intentionally include others of different traditions, church sizes, and ethnic or racial origins. Covenant
  groups should be open to anyone who feels a personal
  need to become a participant.
- *Consensus.* We make decisions by consensus. We agree
  to disagree, but we will not make a significant decision
  affecting the members of the group unless there is full
  agreement among the members. Leaders in our groups
  facilitate and serve; they do not govern.
- *Process.* Group members must be sensitive to group process. Pastors tend to speak in uninterrupted, thirty-plus-
  minute segments and at the end expect everyone to say,
  "Amen!" What works in the pulpit doesn't work in board

meetings, staff meetings, and especially gatherings of other pastors. As pastors learn how to dialogue with one another (and submit to one another!), they will become more effective with the gifted, outspoken people in their own congregations.

- *Transdenominational.* There is an emerging need among pastors in denominational settings (including pastors of independent evangelical churches) to relate to other Christian leaders outside their own denominations and movements. We think covenant groups should cross denominational and nondenominational lines. We even have groups in which charismatic and Pentecostal leaders are in covenant friendships with those who are not charismatic or Pentecostal. Imagine that!

- *Multiplication without division.* After more than six years of meeting together, we have discovered firsthand why it is so difficult for cell groups in the local church to divide or even to include new people. It takes so much time and energy to build meaningful relationships that people in those relationships are unwilling to start over and exchange them for new ones. We have determined, then, that to start up other groups, two or more must serve as a kind of leadership catalyst for a new group while continuing to participate in the original group. This allows multiplication without division.

Spouses of Group Participants

Possibly one of the more interesting issues we have struggled with is how to include or even whether to include our spouses in our relationships with one another. Here are some of the comments from participants in our initial covenant groups (all men) about the involvement of our spouses in our group activities.

I do not expect my wife to have the same kind of relationship with the wives of the men in my group as I have with those men.

I like the suggestion that everyone in their group should find a counselor for their marriage, for their family, and to report back to the group the specific name of the counselor. That seems like a good safety net.

My wife feels a need herself to connect when we are going through a crisis in the church. She can't vent to people in the church, and few women understand the pressures on the pastor's wife. And the smaller the church, the greater the pressure. My wife can't go to her pastor (me) for help.

I believe my wife needs to know the men of my group have the right to speak into my life on every issue. The men in my group, by my choice, have great power in my life. So I'm looking for a way for my wife to get to know the men in my group.

My wife is generally not interested in knowing my friends. She has her own friends.

Sometimes it really helps me understand the other guys in our group when I see them in the context of their relationship with their wife.

Maybe it would help if we could encourage our wives to get into a group of women who can pray.

The issue is not who's in each group, but whether or not we see the value of a support system, a group, to encourage spouses, to help them, to love and challenge them. Should we not consider encouraging our wives to reach out to form a commitment group? A support system?

Research shows that wives of pastors suffer more than their spouses. They are, perhaps, even more isolated than their husbands who are in the ministry.

And then there's the whole issue of women in ministry, when the wife of the pastor is in ministry with him. My wife is in partnership with me, so she doesn't want to meet with a bunch of "pastor's wives." Just because she's female, she has been excluded from many church and leader meetings that could be so helpful for her.

So, what did we conclude when a number of us discussed this issue? *Nothing!* As you can see from the comments above, no one was quite sure what to do with the issue of including spouses. So on a group-by-group basis, some include wives in dinners or retreats and some don't.

We do know of several women-in-ministry covenant groups that meet on a regular basis, and our group includes our spouses in our annual three-day retreat. Last September we traveled together to Coronado Island across the bay from San Diego. We rode bikes, ate out, walked a lot, played golf, and went boogey boarding in the surf. It was great fun, except for our structured meetings.

On Monday and Tuesday morning we all met in a large suite for morning worship and devotions. Everyone was pleasant, but the men were talking while the women remained quiet. One of the men began our devotional time by talking about how "riding the waves" of the Spirit can get you in trouble. That led into one of our typically loud, heated discussions about theology and church life. After ending our morning gathering with a good prayer, we were off to the business of having fun.

The next morning started out pretty much the same. We worshiped and then began the devotion. Once again the men were out-talking the wives, until my wife, Susan, blurted out, "Is anyone else here feeling left out? I am feeling marginalized by all this church talk."

After a prolonged silence, the other spouses slowly but surely chimed in with comments like:

"All you guys do is talk at each other."
"You don't listen; you just talk."
"What are we doing here?"
"Nobody is sharing anything personal."
"I don't want to keep coming to these retreats if this is all we're going to do."
"Is this what you do when you get together?"

One of the wives even confronted her husband, right there in front of us all, telling him that all he ever does is talk without listening. This led to some lively and surprisingly healthy dialogue about relationships and communication styles. As a result, we men have released the task of planning our next retreat—including the content and focus of our devotional times—to our spouses.

■ The Journey

As we all know, successful pastoral ministry is a journey with ups and downs, twists and turns. Our covenant group is showing us that meaningful relationships are also a journey. Each time we think we have something working, along comes an incident (or our spouses!) to remind us that we still have a lot of work to do.

A friend said, "A lot of discouragement goes on in pastors' lives. The covenant group is a safe place to share with and pray for one another. Real friendships have developed in the groups. These brothers are friends I can count on." In the next chapter, though, I want to tell you what happened in our group when we didn't count on each other.

Building Safe Groups

> I've stayed in ministry because of our group. I wanted out of pastoral ministry just a few years ago, but my group has held me steady.
>
> —PIC group member

"She left today. Went to stay with her sister. I don't know what I should do. I don't think she's coming back."

The call came on Thanksgiving Day from Steve, the pastor of a thriving church in Phoenix. The marital crisis surfaced when he returned from an overseas mission trip only to find his wife more dissatisfied than ever with what she perceived as his lack of attention. "I felt her demands were unrealistic, but I never realized how deeply hurt she was," he told me (Al).

Heated discussions and finger-pointing climaxed with a separation, so Steve took a sabbatical from ministry and worked on putting their marriage back together.

"I've learned a lot through my marriage crisis," Steve said. "I now know that I've been too much of a lone ranger. I need a closer relationship with my wife, and I need friends who can

help me hang in there during personal and organizational difficulties. I need other ministers in my life."

Steve wanted to join a pastors' covenant group but had a lot
of questions. He had participated as a member of a number
of committees and had once served on a denominational task
force, but he had never been part of a group that focused on
personal issues.

■ PIC as One Type of Relational Group

Like Steve, most members of the clergy are isolated and have
little or no experience with deeply personal support groups.
Our Pastors in Covenant group model is not the only way to
develop and sustain relationships. It is, however, one that has
worked for us and continues to work for others. When speaking to Steve about relational groups, I shared with him our
PIC mission statement:

> To develop a fellowship of local Christian leaders with a de-
> fined membership that promotes pastoral health and excellence
> through peer friendships, nurture, and support.

Notice the main focus is on peer friendships, nurture, and
support. We believe Pastors in Covenant groups provide a safe
environment in which members can:

- foster sustainable friendships with other pastors and
  ministry executives
- receive mutual support in solving personal and professional problems
- increase competence in the fundamental practices of
  ministry
- be accountable to friends they trust to help them manage in a healthy manner the problems and issues they
  face in ministry

Whatever you call your group—a covenant group, support group, or friendship group—there are essential elements of group life that must be carefully considered and embraced.

Safety First

Recently a task force for a major denomination reviewed the challenges of pastoral ministry today and concluded that pastors need *safe places, safe times,* and *safe people* in which to confront and overcome those challenges. Without a relationally safe place where people are both challenged and loved, growth and change cannot occur.

In Henry Cloud and John Townsend's *Safe People Workbook,* they list a number of personal traits of "unsafe people." Here are fourteen of them.[1]

1. Unsafe people think they "have it all together" instead of admitting their weaknesses.
2. Unsafe people are religious instead of spiritual.
3. Unsafe people are defensive instead of open to feedback.
4. Unsafe people are self-righteous instead of humble.
5. Unsafe people only apologize instead of changing their behavior.
6. Unsafe people avoid working on their problems instead of dealing with them.
7. Unsafe people demand trust instead of earning it.
8. Unsafe people believe they are perfect instead of admitting their faults.
9. Unsafe people blame others instead of taking responsibility themselves.
10. Unsafe people lie instead of telling the truth.
11. Unsafe people are stagnant instead of growing.
12. Unsafe people avoid closeness instead of connecting.
13. Unsafe people flatter us instead of confronting us.
14. Unsafe people gossip instead of keeping secrets.

These fourteen traits can be used to help us describe safe people and safe groups as well.

1. Safe people don't think they "have it all together" and willingly admit their weaknesses. Safe groups are places where people can confess their shortcomings.
2. Safe people are spiritual, not religious. Safe groups foster spiritual formation, not religious artificiality.
3. Safe people are open to feedback and are not defensive. Safe groups offer feedback that is received by the members.
4. Safe people are humble and resist being self-righteous. Safe groups embrace weakness, and members seek the needed grace to change.
5. Safe people apologize for wrongdoing and change their behavior. Safe groups focus on change and accountability.
6. Safe people work on their problems. In safe groups members admit to problems and work on them.
7. Safe people earn trust and don't demand it. Safe groups grow in trust.
8. Safe people admit their faults and believe they are not perfect. Safe groups are transparent and authentic; members share their shortcomings.
9. Safe people take responsibility for their own actions and do not blame others. Safe groups have a high level of personal responsibility and accountability.
10. Safe people tell the truth; they don't lie. Safe groups risk speaking the truth in love.
11. Safe people are always growing, never stagnant. In safe groups members continue to show positive change over time.
12. Safe people connect with other safe people. In safe groups, members bond to each other and become friends.
13. Safe people challenge and affirm one another and are not patronizing. Believing that "iron sharpens iron," safe groups are graciously confrontational.
14. Safe people don't gossip. Safe groups are places where confidentiality is a high value.

Having a safe place of acceptance and nurture is an essential human need. Those in full-time Christian ministry are no different from the people who come to them for ministry. Yet so many of the sheep God entrusts to a pastor's care act more like wolves! Biting sheep are an occupational hazard of Christian ministry, the effect of which must be overcome with liberal doses of love and friendship from those whom we trust. As one group member shared, in a time of church dysfunction and pain, a safe group or friend is a healing balm. "I've been in the pastorate for fifteen years and have never had such hurt and pain as this. I didn't realize how easily people you've helped can turn against you. It has been a healing experience for me to have you friends."

The Risk of "Unsafe People"

Being a pastor is often unsafe, because clergy are in the business of helping "unsafe people." After all, aren't the needy, hurting, and sinful people of this world our harvest field?

A number of years ago I (Al) made an extraordinary personal investment of time and love in the life of someone who later turned on me. Jesus told us that this kind of thing would happen to those in ministry. Loving people is a risk! Yet I still found it difficult to reconcile how the individual I had prayed for, counseled, and cared about could turn around and maliciously attack me. At that time I read a *Transactional Analysis Bulletin* article by Stephen Karpman that helped me greatly. I've adapted the author's model for people in ministry. Picture the pastor at the top point of a triangle, the needy congregant at the bottom left, and the person's painful past at the bottom right.

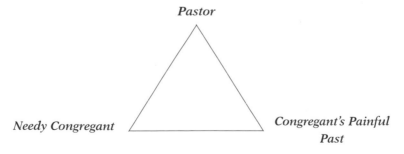

Pastor

Needy Congregant

Congregant's Painful Past

As we discussed earlier, much of the difficulty of ministry is rooted in the unrealistic expectations people have for us. When pastors reach out to wounded people, those they are helping will value deeply both their counsel and attention. People in church not only look to their spiritual leaders for help; they look up to them too. The mantle of spiritual authority can be dangerous as well as powerful.

This element of the pastor-member relationship is a potential minefield of misunderstandings. Problems can emerge, for example, when the pastor is, for whatever reason, no longer able to meet the expectations of the person receiving his or her ministry. Perhaps the Christian leader simply doesn't know what to do, or because of a busy personal schedule isn't able to give the hurting believer the time and attention he or she was hoping for. Or perhaps the person was coming to the pastor for affirmation and support and—gasp!—the pastor corrected them instead!

Or worse, the church member discovers, as a result of some incident—it could be a relatively minor one—just how human the pastor and his family really are! All of a sudden, it seems, the one being helped, the one who so appreciated the pastor's love and insight, is complaining to other people in the church. Or not going to church! As we have illustrated in figure 9.1, the pastor has become part of a "vicious triangle."

This is why many a sheep bites the hand that feeds it and why people leave churches. They want, need, and thrive on the attention, acceptance, and affirmation they receive from their pastor. They want to be affirmed, appreciated, and loved. They want what they may never have, or perhaps lost, from a parental/authority figure.

To keep the affirmation coming their way, they may keep telling their pastor how much they appreciate him or her, how much God touched them through the pastor's words, and how they want to be the pastor's friend. In their gratefulness they may even treat the pastor to dinners out or give their pastor a nice gift. When the pastor is unable or unwilling to meet their expectations, though, they become angry, even vindictive, and strike out or leave the church. Professional caregivers are usually schooled in the dangers of becoming too close to a client, but I have found that these counselor-client dynamics are not commonly understood by people in Christian ministry.

The lesson in this is that pastors will inevitably find it hard to have safe, healthy relationships within their fellowship of congregants. Many people in the church have great personalities and willing hearts but are not safe people. If you become too close to them, the relationship may well backfire. You have a far better chance of finding a safe place with peers, especially in a group setting. A healthy group dynamic diffuses the idolatry-to-disrespect cycle and promotes safety through numbers and intentional relationship.

Keep It Confidential

"Safe people don't gossip. Safe groups are places where confidentiality is a high value." This statement from the above list of traits of safe people and groups is crucial. Groups discuss intimate and often harrowing aspects of people's lives. If these details are made known to others outside the group—spouses, friends, other clergy—the aggrieved victim could rightly declare that his or her trust had been broken, and trust is the essential component of a safe relationship. One will not feel safe if trust has not been built or maintained.

I often think of trust as the result of regular deposits of faithfulness, honesty, care, and concern into the relationship bank. A single significant violation of confidentiality can result in a withdrawal that leaves one's trust account overdrawn. This is what happens with adultery in a marriage, which can leave the relationship bankrupt. Where there is a serious breech of trust, repeated acts of faithfulness, loyalty, and caring are needed to restore the trust account. Groups become safe as trust is built over long periods of time. They remain safe through confidentiality, but a single slip of the tongue can destroy that trust.

■ Our Experience with Personal Support Groups

In a recent meeting of a national denominational steering committee, the subject came up of how to effectively structure pastoral support groups. All believed in the power of groups to promote pastoral excellence and character growth, but not surprisingly, only a couple of the thirty people present had any personal experience with groups. As a consultant, I was asked to talk about the things we have learned about groups. In this section I want to share some of these with you.

Group size. Our initial Pastors in Covenant group has nine members. We think this is a bit large, but as I previously mentioned, no one wants to leave. Four to seven members is a much better size. I am also part of another leadership growth group. Four of us meet monthly for an evening followed by breakfast the next morning. Generally speaking, the larger the group the more difficult it is to build the all-important sense of "groupness."

A larger group also affords less time for participation by each member and therefore takes members longer to connect and build trust. Furthermore, more talkative members are likely to dominate, and there is a greater likelihood that subgroups will form.

On the other hand, a group that is too small (two or three) can have distinct disadvantages as well. There is less opportunity for people to meet others who seem to them interesting, confirming, or compatible. Smaller groups also have more difficulty functioning when members are absent. Finally, a small group will not contain the variety of experience members may need from one another. So, as with most things, a size somewhere in the middle seems to be the best.

Leadership. Every group needs a leader or facilitator. The success of a group is substantially dependent on who leads it. The role of the facilitator is not to control the group, but to assist the members in developing connection, care, and relationship. Group leaders must realize their role is one of servanthood, not governance. The role of a facilitator is to guide the group, not control it. The leader enforces the group's self-determined rules and boundaries, not his or her own.

The facilitator is also the communication and scheduling contact for the group. For example, in my group I am now the designated facilitator. I have the job of keeping the meeting moving in a direction that encourages sharing, listening, and connection. We have developed a few rules (see chapter 8) to help keep us focused. When I am absent from the meeting, I designate someone else to lead the group.

A facilitator who talks too much or is dominant or bossy will negatively influence the group. One who doesn't make sure interactions are appropriate and is passive will not provide needed direction and structure. Mainly, what I do as a facilitator in our group is keep the shoptalk from overshadowing the heart talk.

We have found it helpful to give everyone in our group an opportunity to facilitate our meetings. Gary's second group, for example, meets at a different church each month so that members of the covenant group have an opportunity to see and "feel" the ministries of the people in the group. Whoever hosts the meeting is the designated facilitator.

Location and setting. As we said earlier, our covenant group meets in a converted guesthouse in the prayer garden of a large church. We all love it. Other groups meet in homes, while still others meet in church offices that are comfortable and private. That's the key: comfortable and private.

We all sit around a large oak table where we are able to see each other and share. Other groups sit comfortably on couches or chairs facing each other. The setup needs to be conducive to heartfelt communication without the interruption of people or phones. Busy people are always in demand, so cell phones need to be off during group meeting time.

Meeting time. One group I am part of meets for an evening through breakfast the next morning. One member, the leader of a large recovery ministry, lives an hour and a half out of Phoenix. He lives alone since his wife divorced him a few years ago. Two other friends—one a major league baseball scout, the other the head of a large and influential Christian ministry—and I join him at his home once a month for food and fellowship. We meet there together, share a meal, spend the night, and leave the next morning.

As we said earlier, our PIC group meets three hours the first Thursday of every month. Other covenant groups in our network meet every two weeks. Some even meet weekly. We think that three hours a month together is a minimum. We also recommend that groups meet for no less than an hour and a half, because it takes time to reengage and then to go deeper. The important thing is that the time is a scheduled appointment—otherwise it just won't happen in our busy lives.

Building trust. Don't assume that trust will just happen if people meet and share. This is only partially true. Trust has to be nurtured in an environment of love, acceptance, and affirmation over long periods of time. We trust others when we have relied on them and they have proven themselves worthy of our trust. We place confidence in those we trust. This is why I believe that trust, though certainly an element of faith, is somewhat different.

Faith is often supernaturally imparted as well as personally developed through study and reading of the Word of God. On the other hand, I think of trust as an emotional response that grows through life experiences. When God allows a difficult time in our life and proves his faithfulness to us, we learn to trust him more. God's grace to us in the trials of life cultivate within us an emotional response of trust in him and a growing confidence when new trials come. We become less fearful and more trusting with each trial he brings us through.

Trust grows in our relationships with each other much the same way. The more we connect and depend on each other through difficult life issues, the more we can trust each other. There are, however, three essential components of the trust-building process: authentic transparency, empathic listening, and nondefensive responding.

Authentic transparency. Being authentic means being actually and exactly who you are. Transparency is the absence of pretense. You allow others to see you the way God sees you—just the way you are. This is a big risk! To be transparent is to be vulnerable, but to be vulnerable is to be credible.

Personally, I have found it hard to be authentically transparent with my groups and friends, because I feared they would think less of me if they knew what I was "really like." This is probably the great challenge for any person and therefore any relationship. Biblically speaking, it's sin that separates us from God and one another, and healing comes only when we confess our sins, when we are honest and open about who we really are and extend forgiveness and acceptance to one another as God does to us.

When a person is authentically transparent, he or she will feel terribly vulnerable and risk rejection, yet this is what intimacy and connection are all about. Genesis 2:18–25 is God's blueprint for significant relationships. Verse 25 reads, "The man and his wife were both naked, and they felt no shame."

The Hebrew word translated "naked" here implies not only physical nakedness, but emotional nakedness as well. The Hebrew root of the word translated "ashamed" may also be translated "disappointed." So, to paraphrase, "The man and his wife were both transparent and were not disappointed when they saw each other exactly as they were." The foundation of true intimacy is being authentically transparent in a relationship and not being rejected for it. Group closeness and trust are not built until someone risks being authentically transparent.

Empathic listening. To have empathy is to be sensitive to the feelings, thoughts, and experiences of another. It means being compassionate and understanding. Empathy is feeling what others feel, bearing one another's burdens. Jesus is our empathetic high priest who is "touched by the feelings of our infirmities." When we are able to empathize, our verbal and nonverbal messages communicate love and acceptance, not disappointment and rejection.

Compassionately listening to someone share his or her pain and sin conveys acceptance of the person. Consider doing the following to let the other person know you are listening:

- Focus on the person when he or she shares. Lean forward, not backward.
- Maintain a comfortable level of eye contact.
- Summarize what you hear the person saying.
- Ask questions but not rhetorical ones.
- Nod your head in understanding.
- Keep an open body posture.

Nondefensive responding. Not only do we need to listen to others when they share their lives, but we must also listen to the feedback we invite. This has been a big issue in my family of origin. When we were growing up, no one ever seemed to listen. I come from an Irish-Spanish Catholic family of eight children, six of whom are boys. We were always jostling, teasing, and shouting over each other's comments. It was not a healthy climate for sharing heartfelt issues or appropriately receiving feedback.

My mother, however, is a different story. She is a gifted listener and nondefensive responder to criticism or feedback. Her confidence in relationships has challenged my less healthy patterns. As much as anything, I've had to work on not being defensive when my wife gives me feedback. She might say that after many years of working on this area of my life I've improved somewhat! Last year a good friend complimented me on how very well I took criticism. That was nice to hear, but unfortunately it seems like I'm much more willing to listen to others than I am willing to respond to my wife.

Defensiveness is a style of responding to feedback, criticism, or contempt from another wherein the responder is more interested in defending himself or herself than listening and problem solving. John Gottman provides some examples of relationally defensive behaviors in his book *Why Marriages Succeed or Fail*:

- Denying responsibility: "It wasn't my fault."
- Making excuses: "I couldn't help being late."
- Cross-complaining: Your spouse: "We never go out anymore." Your response: "Well, you never want to make love."
- Rubber man/rubber woman: Your partner: "You don't listen to me." Your response: "Well, you don't listen to me."
- Yes-butting: "Yeah, we could try that, but I don't think it will work."
- Repeating yourself: "That's what I have been trying to tell you over and over again."
- Whining: "Why are you picking on me?"
- Explaining self: "Here's why I did this. I was just trying to . . ."
- Body language: hands folded across chest, looking the other way, etc.[2]

My wife, Susan, would tell you that I have used every one of these defenses at some time in my life. I knew a pastor (now deceased) who was known for his gracious response to feedback and criticism. When approached by another, he would listen attentively, and if the feedback struck a chord with him, he would thank the person and respond with, "That sounds right for me." If it didn't immediately register, he would still thank the person and say, "I'll pray about that and get back to you." He always did.

■ Summing It Up

Most of us in ministry are isolated, so intentional friendships are essential. Though many of us may chose to develop relationships one at a time, doing so in a group has many advantages. Many of the people we minister to are hurting, immature, and "unsafe." Peer friendships, then, can make all the difference, because others in ministry understand fully the unique demands on one who is in full-time Christian work, and they can empathize.

Peer friendships for life are cultivated when we hear and are being heard. Listening, receiving, and graciously responding to another's input, especially when everything inside us is crying out in self-defense, is good for us!

Lessons Learned

"Greater love has no one than this, that he lay down his life for
his friends."

—John 15:13

It's a myth that accountability can occur outside of community.

—Michael Card

It has been almost four years, but I (Al) remember it like
yesterday. I put down the telephone receiver and turned to
my wife, Susan, and said, "Ann just left Bill (not their real
names). She has rented an apartment and moved out. I just
can't believe it!"

Bill is my friend and an original member of our first Pastors
in Covenant group. His wife, a gifted woman, was the worship minister at their nine-hundred-member denominational
church. The two had traveled all over the world conducting
marriage conferences. Bill was a sought-after itinerant preacher
before retiring from travel and settling down to pastor. They
were a dynamic, charming couple, and the church doubled in

157

size within just a few years of Bill becoming the senior minister. Future opportunities looked great for even more significant ministry, but then came the crash.

What went wrong? I just couldn't accept the fact that their marriage was failing. I also had a hard time understanding why our covenant group seemed to have dropped the ball. Bill and I exchanged a lot of phone calls during that period.

"What about counseling?" I would ask. " Are you sure this is for the best? Is Ann willing to talk to me? What does your son, Matt, think? What's going to happen to Andy?"

It seemed like no matter what I said or did, nothing changed. They were separated, and divorce was imminent. I talked to a few of the guys in our group. They were incredulous, confused. And they were angry. One or two in our group of nine had phoned Bill, but he hadn't returned their calls.

Members of our group asked, "How could Bill have been going through such a difficult time and not shared it with us? We didn't have a clue this was happening! How come he didn't tell us?"

When I talked to Bill, he poured out his overwhelming sense of despair and pain. He had felt compelled to resign his church, so he not only lost his wife, but his ministry as well. Few people knew that two weeks after his wife left, his sixteen-year-old severely handicapped son, Andy, almost died twice. Andy ended up in the intensive care unit of a local hospital for nine weeks. In some ways, this was more devastating for Bill than the crisis in his marriage. Andy required total care, and Bill had been his main caregiver. Everything precious in Bill's life was seemingly being ripped away.

To make matters worse, Bill's church was in such shock that only one of the many men he had encouraged and discipled called him. The rest of the congregants were conspicuously silent. Even the board of elders didn't seem to know what to do with Bill's abrupt departure, which provoked terrible misunderstandings regarding Bill's compensation and severance. Bill and Ann were such prominent and powerful leaders that this was the last thing anybody expected. One church member friend confided in me that she didn't know who to call or what to say, since she saw them both as pastoral leaders and friends and didn't know how to contact one without seeming to be against the other. Most of the church probably felt the same way.

Furthermore, Bill and his covenant group members became increasingly upset with one another. Both sides felt betrayed. Bill quit coming to our group meetings immediately after Ann moved out. He spent long days and nights at the hospital caring for Andy. The group, on the other hand, felt that Bill had never openly shared his problems; in fact, no one in the group had any sense that Bill's life was in such crisis until after his wife left and Bill resigned his position at the church.

We thought Bill had serious friendships in the group, but he made no effort to ask any of us for counsel before leaping into his life-altering decisions. Yet Bill was stung that the group hadn't reached out to him! I was a recent newcomer to the group, joining just after Bill quit coming. I saw a brother in trouble, a man isolating himself from others because of his pain and shame, while friends stood by waiting for him to come to them.

"I don't need friends like that," Bill would say. "Not one of them was there when I needed him. Why should I give any of them the time of day?"

Have you ever been in a similar situation, one in which you could see both sides of the grievance? As a newcomer to our group, I felt I had a clearer, more objective picture of the situation than Bill or the men in covenant. I felt I had to do something to bring about reconciliation and healing. After all, these guys, certainly less than perfect friends, were friends nevertheless and Christian brothers. Moreover, they were leaders in the body of Christ! It was bad enough that a marriage couldn't be saved. A falling out with friends and colleagues would only make matters much worse. So I confronted the group. "He's the hurting brother. You can't expect him to do it right. You have to go the extra mile and reach out to him. Let's invite him to a group meeting and talk."

The group agreed. Initially Bill wasn't ready. He was still smarting. A week or two later his heart opened and he agreed to meet. "I'm not really angry with them," he confessed. "I feel more embarrassed and ashamed that I have let everyone down by not being able to keep my marriage together and my ministry working."

■ The Day We All Talked

Bill sheepishly entered the room. He was obviously nervous and self-conscious. After all, he was in a closed room with eight of his closest peers, men who understood the serious implications of provoking a church crisis because of unresolved marriage problems. I felt anxiety in our group as well. It was hard to face a fellow minister who had failed, one they knew so personally.

Bill broke the silence. "I am sorry I let you all down," he stammered.

"Why didn't you tell us you were having problems?" "Why didn't you come to us for help?" asked people in our group.

Bill shared how the serious problem had become apparent while he was busy in ministry overseas. Perhaps because he was such a great distance from home, the growing emotional chasm between him and his wife became painfully obvious. Returning home, an immediate crisis with his wife led to a whirlwind separation and divorce. Bill's world turned upside down, and he never returned to the group—until this day.

When Bill broke down and wept, Ron was the first in our group to respond: "I am so sorry I let you down, brother. Please forgive me for not reaching out and helping you in your time of need." More tears. Others apologized in turn. We huddled around Bill. We prayed, and God brought about an extraordinary healing and reconciliation.

■ Lessons Learned

Did the group fail Bill? I think so. Did Bill fail his friends? Yes, I think he did. Does that mean that the group itself failed in what it is supposed to be, a place of commitment to friendship where we can walk together and "bear one another's burdens and so fulfill the law of Christ" (Gal. 6:2 KJV)?

Some of you reading this will probably say yes, and for good reason. Some members of our group may agree, but I'm less willing to judge too quickly any one of us or all of us. In the end, it was evident that the men in our group had genuine relationships. Yes, we let each other down. Yes, we didn't handle this well, but relationships are messy. In fact, if there is no conflict in a relationship, deep relationship probably doesn't exist. When people are in crisis, confusion and mishandling of relationships are inevitable. If you love someone, sooner or later you will likely hurt them. Good relationship is not the absence of conflict, but a determination and grace to resolve and forgive. Conflict is common. Godly resolution of conflict is uncommon.

■ It's All about Jesus

The closer you are to another the more likely there will be failure at some point in your relationship—and the greater the need for Jesus. He was the one who compelled me to reach out to Bill and my group. I even sensed he was facilitating the group the day we all met. He softened our hearts and brought compassion, understanding, and forgiveness. He healed the breach.

Jesus was the key to the healing, the redemption of the failure, and the restoring of fellowship. He is the Good Shepherd who leaves the flock to go out and find the one bruised, hurt, or missing lamb (Matt. 18:12–14). I think our experience made us understand a little more of what Jesus is like and what he expects of us in relationships. Relationship is his creation, not ours. I don't know that any of us in our group will neglect to take the initiative the next time one of us falters.

■ What to Do When Others Seem to Be Failing

We can't emphasize enough this reality: When ministry leaders are in trouble or hurting, they will not respond perfectly to the challenge or crisis. The emotions, the pain, the fears in difficult times are simply too great. Many will also not reach out for help either. They will be too absorbed with their own pain and shame. Those of us who are friends of persons in pain must not take it personally. It is not about us, it is about them and their personal struggle.

The apostle James tells us that when there is a sick person among us, we should call for the elders of the church to pray (James 5:14–16). *Their* prayer of faith will heal the sick. Yes, it certainly adds to the healing power of faith when the sick person expects a healing too, but James is teaching us that the person who needs prayer cannot make it alone. Often others must take the initiative.

When a leader is in crisis, church boards and elders will only rarely know precisely how to work everyone through the conflict. Fear, anger, disappointment, and even resentment are common. Congregants will be hurt and confused. They will be "sheep without a shepherd." Even other leaders in the city will not know if they should call, intervene, or just pray. Some will even use the crisis as an opportunity to announce, "I told you so. I knew this would happen." When the shepherd is stricken everybody suffers!

What would Jesus do? What should we do?

First, be real about who you are and don't indirectly or directly set up false expectations. You are the jars of clay, cracks and all, not the treasure (2 Cor. 4:7). This doesn't mean you have to confess every sin publicly, but it does mean you need to live an *authentic* life. Bill and Ann were "larger than life" to the people in their church. This means that people did not expect them ever to have problems. "They were so anointed, how could they fail?" a close friend observed. My answer, "Easily. We are all sinners saved by grace."

Dialogue with your leaders ahead of time about how they would handle the crisis of your untimely death, disability, or failure. Doing so is a way of "fail-safing" your ministry. Having a crisis contingency plan and even a succession plan is just being wise. One never knows what tomorrow may bring. As a pastor friend of mine told me, "Prepare for the worst and pray for the best." Don't let the busyness of today keep you from planning for tomorrow.

Be a friend who "loves at all times." When you are in relationship with someone, don't let that person or yourself off the hook. Expect to be a part of your friend's life until he or she tells you not to be or until it is absolutely clear and verified through counsel that you should not be that person's close friend. Treat the friendship as a sacred trust for which you are responsible.

Don't let anger or offenses separate you. We all know the biblical injunctions about offense: "If you are offering your gift at the altar and there remember that your brother has something against you, leave your gift . . . go and be reconciled" (Matt. 5:23). And, "If your brother sins against you, go and show him his fault . . ." (Matt. 18:15–17). Caring enough about the friendship to go to each other is the real test of how well you do relationship. Taking the initiative to heal a relationship is humbling hard work. Ask Jesus.

Talk to your friends ahead of time about what you expect of each other in the relationship. As the saying goes, "An ounce of prevention is worth a pound of cure." For example, one friend and I (Al) have talked about what we would do if we saw the other "doing something dumb." Agreeing ahead of time on how you will handle each other's failure, weakness, and sin, should it occur, gives each member of the relationship the permission to be involved. It makes the expectations clear. It also reduces potential confusion and offense, because we know what to expect of each other.

Invite accountability ahead of time. Accountability is best understood as inviting another to hold you to your word regarding an issue in your life. Accountability is not something anyone can impose, but when it is invited, it becomes a natural part of friendship and community. I (Gary), for example, have asked, even begged, significant people in my life—my adult children, my colleagues and close friends, the executive committee of my board—to correct and challenge me when my behaviors are not appropriate or godly. I have discovered, however, that surprisingly few people make themselves open and vulnerable to such counsel and correction.

Another way to look at accountability is to see it in the context of protection. Bill Thrall believes that protection is the primary value of accountability. It releases hope, because when we are in an accountable, protected relationship, we don't have to hide anymore. In addition to our own resources, we have those of another who cares.

When trouble, difficulty, or impending failure strikes, go to your friend. Don't expect your friend to come to you. Call him, talk to him, listen to him, and offer your prayers and support. And keep calling, listening, and praying. You may need to do this for years! When bad things happen to good friends, the repercussions often last years, not days or months.

I (Al) continue to talk with my friend about how he is doing after the pain of divorce two years ago following thirty-seven years of marriage. It is unrealistic to think that the wound would be healed from that kind of trauma in a matter of weeks or months. He still sees his wife on occasion, and the pain simply will not go away.

Your spouse should be your best but not only close friend. Corey and his wife, who have known each other from childhood, have pioneered a ministry together and are best friends. He told me he didn't see much need for more friends. I tried to convince him that there are church challenges that could be better met if he had close friends other than his wife. I asked him, for example, what would happen if they both came under attack. Who was going to remain objective? Who was going to have the strength to support the other in a healthy manner?

In addition, every marriage has its relational dynamics. In a crisis the dynamic of their intimate marital relationship will dictate their response unless there is also external, trusted counsel from a friend. Corey is now interested in starting a group of peers.

■ Do You Want to Start a Group?

Starting a group can be much easier than you think. Gary has started three: a couples group and two pastors' covenant groups. Over the years Al has also initiated three groups. Any one person (or two or three friends) can start a group.

Consider starting with friends or friends of friends, people you think would be interested or who are in need. Take someone out to lunch or agree to meet in some casual setting to explore the possibilities. A group won't start without someone taking the initiative to make it happen. Many leaders have expressed an interest in developing peer friendship groups, but few have taken the lead in contacting others and getting a group started.

There are at least three qualifications for starting a group:

1. Someone who has the respect of other ministers in his/her area.
2. Someone who will commit to the group and help sustain it.
3. Someone who is "safe" and therefore open to what group life is all about.

Furthermore, when asking others to form a group with you, look for:

1. Someone you already know, an existing relationship/ friendship.
2. Diversity, that is, someone who is different from you, someone who can offer an alternative perspective in the area of race, denomination, or church size.

After a few of you (two or more) agree to meet regularly, it would be helpful to convene an organizational meeting or even a preliminary retreat to define expectations. You may find it helpful to use an external facilitator for your first couple of meetings or retreats, something our first group found to be invaluable. When organizing, consider the following:

- *Identify a facilitator.* The facilitator is the one responsible for ensuring that the meeting stays on track, that preachers don't preach, and that everyone is heard. We also suggest at least a simple agenda for the format of your meeting. The role of the facilitator is not to dominate conversation, but to encourage everyone else to share. Using a different facilitator for every meeting is not a good idea. The group will work best if you select someone to act as facilitator for six to twelve months then give someone else a turn.

- *Use our covenant or develop your own.* We strongly believe that a covenant is essential. A covenant is a statement clearly defining expectations to which *everyone* agrees. The word *covenant* means different things to different people. Make sure you spend time defining what it means for your group. Here's ours:

Our Covenant

1. Membership is voluntary.
2. Membership is by invitation only to a limited number of people for a twelve-month period.
3. Membership is inclusive of different ethnic groups, Christian traditions, and expressions of faith. A member may invite another to participate under the terms of our agreement, but the group must agree together that the invitee and the timing are appropriate.
4. Transparency with each other is necessary. Open, honest, and healthy relationships begin with the willingness to be vulnerable.
5. Listening is essential. Advice and prayer are invited, not forced.
6. Confidentiality is required. What is shared in covenant groups is not shared elsewhere.
7. Commitment to the following is expected of each group member:
   •willing to be present for 9 of 12 monthly meetings
   •doctrinal accountability to the Apostles' Creed
   •personal and professional accountability as defined in the Pastoral Epistles

---

- *Determine the ideal size of your group.* The size of your group makes a big difference in the intimacy factor. The larger the group, the more complex the relationships and the more difficult for people to share personal issues. Small groups won't have enough dialogue and interchange. As we've mentioned earlier, an ideal group size is four to seven. This number allows for some diversity of people and opinions without being too cumbersome or time-consuming to manage. Some groups may start with three or four members and then decide later to add others.

- *Choose a meeting time and place.* Meeting in a restaurant or public facility won't work well. A private home or very comfortable office works best. Make sure that there are no distractions (telephones, children, etc.), and consider having refreshments. Meeting for an hour or so once a month will not give enough time for the group to connect. Three hours once a month is probably the minimum.

- *Talk about what is going to happen.* Generally and specifically describe what you want to happen in each meeting. Will you discuss only personal issues or professional issues as well? Will your meeting be a forum for ideas? Remember, relationships will grow in any setting like this, but personal health grows when we focus on personal issues, not just on better ideas for our churches and ministries.

- *Explore how you will make your group a "safe" place.* As we said earlier, safety is of great importance in developing trust. Being able to share what makes a group safe for you will clarify expectations and give everyone a better chance of fulfilling the group's goal to cultivate safe friendships.

- *Dialogue about confidentiality.* If you don't establish confidentiality, somebody, sooner or later, will be offended that the group leaked. Obviously, when that happens, people will become less willing to share sensitive issues. Confidentiality makes the group safe.

- *Discuss what would make someone inappropriate for your group.* Review the fourteen characteristics of unsafe people. Perhaps there are some of those kinds of people you especially want to avoid having in your group. The needs of an individual in the group must not overshadow the well-being of the whole group. *Our covenant groups are not therapy groups!* Perhaps some people should not be in your group. The intimacy developed in a covenant group is best handled when men meet with men, women with women, and couples with couples.

- *Explore the issue of personal accountability.* Do you agree that anyone can ask anyone else in the group any question about his or her personal or professional life?

- *Discuss when feedback should be given and how it should be done.* What role should listening play in the group dynamic? A good question to ask is: "Are you asking for advice, or do you just want us to listen and pray?" Christian leaders are good at telling but struggle with the Scripture that says, "Be quick to listen, slow to speak" (James 1:19). Often when we are having problems, we need people just to hear us without them feeling the need to give advice.

- *Break up into smaller groups.* You may occasionally want to break up into smaller groups or even into pairs to build a more intimate connection and give those who may be less inclined to share in a group a safe opportunity.

■ Being a Friend

Friendship may be defined many different ways. Webster says that a friend is "one attached to another, a favored companion." But a dictionary definition lacks the depth, quality, and marvelous adventure that characterize our experience with special people in our lives. Friends and friendship have literally changed us, making us the people we are. Friends have made us better than we ever would have been without them.

Gary and I have shared a lot of laughs, good times, and savory dinners with each other and our friends. We have also experienced pain and tears together. And we are certainly better for it. Our friends have been gifts from God. The impact of their love and influence has drawn us closer to God and helped us be more successful in ministry and leadership.

Jerry and Mary White, in their book *Friends and Friendship*, tell us that intimate friends "are the few people to whom we pour out our souls, sharing our deepest feelings and hopes. They meet us at our point of deepest need, and we enjoy and look forward to being with them above all others. These friendships have a lasting quality which develops over months and years."[1] We pray that you will have many of these kinds of friends.

Notes

Chapter 1: Am I Crazy?

1. *Pastor's Weekly Briefing* 7, no. 7 (12 February 1999): 1–2.
2. As cited by Greg Sullivan in the online feature "Maximized Training," *Group*, <http://www.groupmag.com/past_feature/max_train.asp>.
3. Fuller Institute of Church Growth, 1991.
4. Eugene Peterson in Larry Crabb, *The Safest Place on Earth* (Nashville: Word, 1999), vii.
5. Ibid., cover flap.
6. Fuller Institute of Church Growth, 1991.
7. H. B. London, *Ministries Today*, January 2000.
8. *Pastor's Weekly Briefing*, 2.
9. C. Peter Wagner, *ChurchQuake!* (Ventura, Calif.: Regal, 1999).

Chapter 2: These Guys Are in Trouble!

1. George Barna, *The Index of Leading Spiritual Indicators* (Dallas: Word, 1996), 46.
2. Fuller Institute of Church Growth, 1991.
3. Focus on the Family, 1998.
4. Fuller Institute of Church Growth, 1991.
5. Herbert Freudenberger, *When Helping Starts to Hurt* (Garden City, N.Y.: Doubleday, 1985), 9.
6. Fuller Institute of Church Growth, 1991.
7. Focus on the Family, 1998.

8. Barna, *Index of Leading Spiritual Indicators.*
9. Fuller Institute of Church Growth, 1991.

Chapter 3: The Perfect Church

1. To that I say, "If you don't run the church like a business, you will probably run it like a bad business."
2. Fuller Institute of Church Growth, 1991.
3. John C. LaRue Jr., "Forced Exits," *Leadership* 42 (March/April 1996): 72.
4. Christian A. Schwarz, *Natural Church Development: A Guide to Eight Essential Qualities of Healthy Churches* (Carol Stream, Ill.: ChurchSmart Resources, 1996).

Chapter 4: On Being Human

1. George Barna, personal correspondence, July 9, 2003.
2. Ibid.
3. Rick Warren, *The Purpose-Driven Life* (Grand Rapids: Zondervan, 2002), 176.
4. Daniel Goleman, *Primal Leadership: Realizing the Power of Emotional Intelligence* (Boston: Harvard Business School Press, 2002), 102.

Chapter 5: Modeling Failure

1. You may want to visit his website, www.notalone.org.
2. Margaret Carlson, "A President Finds His Voice," *Time,* 24 September 2001, 50.
3. Goleman, *Primal Leadership,* 47.
4. Mary D. Moller, "Meeting the Spiritual Needs in an Inpatient Unit," *Journal of Psychosocial Nursing* (November 1999): 5ff.
5. Paul D. Stanley and J. Robert Clinton, *Connecting: The Mentoring Relationships You Need to Succeed in Life* (Colorado Springs: NavPress, 1992), 159.

Chapter 6: Al Saved My Life

1. Gary Kinnaman, *Overcoming the Dominion of Darkness* (Grand Rapids: Chosen, 1990), republished by Servant Books in 2003 as *Winning Your Spiritual Battles: How to Put On the Full Armor of God.*
2. My thanks to Len Griffin, Daryl Vander Haar, Hal Sacks, Ed D'Avola, Chris Wolfard, Bob Blayter, Dr. Bill Hamon, Dean Sherman, and Dr. Bill Retts.
3. For information, visit www.profilesinternational.com
4. Bill Hybels, *Courageous Leadership* (Grand Rapids: Zondervan, 2002), 184.
5. Philip Gourevitch, "Pol Pot's Children," *New Yorker* 74, no. 23 (10 August 1998): 40–53.
6. Daniel Goleman, *Primal Leadership: Realizing the Power of Emotional Intelligence* (Boston: Harvard Business School Press, 2002), 93, 95.
7. Ibid., 108.
8. Hybels, *Courageous Leadership,* 248–49.
9. Stanley and Clinton, *Connecting,* 159, italics mine.

Chapter 7: Friendships for Life

1. Goleman, *Primal Leadership*, 6–7, italics mine.
2. Ralph Keyes, *We the Lonely People* (New York: HarperCollins, 1973), italics mine.
3. Robert Putnam, *Bowling Alone* (New York: Simon & Schuster, 2000).
4. Ibid., 204. I also recommend an excellent collection of essays on the value of staying in one place, *Staying Put*, by Scott Russell Sanders (Boston: Beacon Press, 1994).
5. Ibid., 223ff.
6. Ibid., 298, 300, 303, 309, 311, 330, 356.

Chapter 9: Building Safe Groups

1. Henry Cloud and John Townsend, *Safe People Workbook* (Grand Rapids: Zondervan, 1995), 17–30.
2. John Gottman, *Why Marriages Succeed or Fail* (New York: Simon & Schuster, 1994), 89–90.

Chapter 10: Lessons Learned

1. Jerry White and Mary White, *Friends and Friendship* (Colorado Springs: NavPress, 1982), 37.

Gary Kinnaman (M.A. in Theology, Fuller; D.Min., Western Conservative Baptist Seminary, Portland) is senior minister of Word of Grace Church (www.wordofgrace.org) in Mesa, Arizona, with a weekend attendance of over forty-five hundred. He is the author of seven books.

Alfred Ells is founder-director of Leaders That Last Ministries, a counseling and leadership development organization for ministers and ministries, and the author of seven books, including *One-Way Relationships*.

For more information on how you can start a Pastors in Covenant group, visit www.pastorsincovenant.org.